Germans

IN MINNESOTA

Kathleen Neils Conzen

Foreword by Bill Holm

MINNESOTA HISTORICAL SOCIETY PRESS

Cover: (front) Betsy, Marge, Sally, Chris, and Jean Didier, granddaughters of immigrants from Prussia and Luxembourg, pause from work on the family farm in St. Martin Township, Stearns County, around 1930; (back) members of the Concordia Singing Society, St. Paul, enjoy a picnic, about 1915.

Publication of this book was supported, in part, with funds provided by the June D. Holmquist Publication Endowment Fund of the Minnesota Historical Society.

www.mnhs.org/mhspress

The Minnesota Historical Society Press is a member of the Association of American University Presses.

Manufactured in Canada

10 9 8 7 6 5 4 3 2 1

International Standard Book Number: 0-87351-454-8

♾ The paper used in this publication meets the minimum requirements of the American National Standard for Information Sciences Permanence for Printed Library Materials, ANSI Z 39.48-1984.

Library of Congress Cataloging-in-Publication Data

Conzen, Kathleen Neils, 1942–
  Germans in Minnesota / Kathleen Neils Conzen ; foreword by Bill Holm.
    p. cm. — (The people of Minnesota)
  Includes bibliographical references and index.
  ISBN 0-87351-454-8 (pbk. : alk. paper)
    1. German Americans—Minnesota—History. 2. German Americans—Minnesota—Social conditions. 3. Minnesota—History. 4. Minnesota—Ethnic relations. I. Minnesota Historical Society. II. Title. III. Series.

F615.G3C66 2003
977.6'00431—dc21

                                2003003924

This book was designed and set in type by Wendy Holdman, Stanton Publication Services, St. Paul, Minnesota; it was printed by Friesens, Altona, Manitoba.

Contents

Foreword

by Bill Holm

Human beings have not been clever students at learning any lessons from their three or four thousand odd years of recorded history. We repeat our mistakes from generation to generation with tedious regularity. But we ought to have learned at least one simple truth: that there is no word, no idea that is not a double-edged sword. Take, for example, the adjective *ethnic*. In one direction, it cuts upward, to show us the faces, the lives, the histories of our neighbors and ourselves. It shows us that we are not alone on this planet—that we are all rooted with deep tendrils growing down to our ancestors and the stories of how they came to be not *there*, but *here*. These tendrils are visible in our noses and cheekbones, our middle-aged diseases and discomforts, our food, our religious habits, our celebrations, our manner of grieving, our very names. The fact that here in Minnesota, at any rate, we mostly live together in civil harmony— showing sometimes affectionate curiosity, sometimes puzzled irritation but seldom murderous violence—speaks well for our progress as a community of neighbors, even as members of a civilized human tribe.

But early in this new century in America we have seen the dark blade of the ethnic sword made visible, and it has cut us to the quick. From at least one angle, our national wounds from terrorist attacks are an example of ethnicity gone mad, tribal loyalty whipped to fanatical hysteria, until it turns human beings into monstrous machines of mass murder. Few tribes own a guiltless history in this regard.

The 20th century did not see much progress toward solving the problem of ethnicity. Think of Turk and Armenian, German and Jew, Hutu and Tutsi, Protestant and Catholic, Albanian and Serb, French and Algerian—think of our own lynchings. We all hoped for better from the 21st century but may not get any reprieve at all from the tidal waves of violence and hatred.

As global capitalism breaks down the borders between nation-states, fanatical ethnicity rises to life like a hydra. Cheerful advertisements assure us that we are all a family—wearing the same pants, drinking the same pop, singing and going on line together as we spend. When we invoke *family,* we don't seen to remember well the ancient Greek family tragedies. We need to make not a family but a civil community of neighbors, who may neither spend nor look alike but share a desire for truthful history—an alert curiosity about the stories and the lives of our neighbors and a respect both for difference—and for privacy. We must get the metaphors right; we are neither brothers nor sisters here in Minnesota, nor even cousins. We are neighbors, all us *ethnics,* and that fact imposes on us a stricter obligation than blood and, to the degree to which we live up to it, makes us civilized.

As both Minnesotans and Americans, none of us can escape the fact that we *ethnics,* in historic terms, have hardly settled here for the length of a sneeze. Most of us have barely had time to lose the language of our ancestors or to produce protein-stuffed children half a foot taller than ourselves. What does a mere century or a little better amount to in history? Even the oldest settlers—the almost ur-inhabitants, the Dakota and Ojibwa—emigrated here from elsewhere on the continent. The Jeffers Petroglyphs in southwest Minnesota are probably the oldest evidence we have of any human habitation. They are still and will most likely remain only shadowy tellers of any historic truth about us. Who made this language? History is silent. The only clear facts scholars agree on about these mysterious pictures carved in hard red Sioux quartzite is that they were the work of neither of the current native tribes and can be scientifically dated only between the melting of the last glacier and the arrival of the first European settlers in the territory. They seem very old to the eye. It is good for us, I think, that our history begins not with certainty, but with mystery, cause for wonder rather than warfare.

In 1978, before the first edition of this ethnic survey appeared, a researcher came to Minneota to interview local people for information about the Icelanders. Tiny though their numbers, the Icelanders were a real ethnic group with their own language, history, and habits of mind. They settled in the late 19th century in three small clumps around Minneota. At that time, I could still introduce this researcher to a few old ladies born in Iceland and to a dozen children of immigrants who grew up with English as a second language, thus with thick accents. The old still prayed the Lord's Prayer in Icelandic, to them the language of Jesus himself, and a handful of people could still read the ancient poems and sagas in the leather-covered editions brought as treasures from the old country. But two decades have wiped out that primary source. The first generation is gone, only a few alert and alive in the second, and the third speaks only English—real Americans in hardly a century. What driblets of Icelandic blood remain are mixed with a little of this, a little of that. The old thorny names, so difficult to pronounce, have been respelled, then corrected for sound.

Is this the end of ethnicity? The complete meltdown into history evaporated into global marketing anonymity? I say no. On a late October day, a letter arrives from a housewife in Nevis, Minnesota. She's never met me, but she's been to Iceland now and met unknown cousins she found on an Internet genealogy search. The didactic voice in my books reminds her of her father's voice: "He could've said that. Are we *all* literary?" We've never met, she confesses, but she gives me enough of her family tree to convince me that we might be cousins fifteen generations back. She is descended, she says with pride, from the Icelandic law speaker in 1063, Gunnar the Wise. She knows now that she is not alone in history. She has shadowing names, even dates, in her very cells. She says—with more smug pride—that her vinarterta (an Icelandic immigrant prune cake that is often the last surviving ghost of the old country) is better than any she ate in Iceland. She invites me to sample a piece if I ever get to Nevis. Who says there is no profit and joy in ethnicity? That killjoy has obviously never tasted vinarterta!

I think what is happening in this letter, both psychologically and culturally, happens simultaneously in the lives of hundreds of thousands of Minnesotans and countless millions of Americans. Only the details differ, pilaf, jiaozi, fry bread, collards, latkes, or menudo rather than vinarterta, but the process and the object remain the same. We came to this cold flat place so far from the sea in wave after wave of immigration—filling up the steadily fewer empty places in this vast midsection of a continent—but for all of us, whatever the reason for our arrival: poverty, political upheaval, ambition—we check most of our history, and thus our inner life, at the door of the new world. For a while, old habits and even the language carry on, but by the third generation, history is lost. Yet America's history, much less Minnesota's, is so tiny, so new, so uncertain, so much composed of broken connections—and now of vapid media marketing—that we feel a loneliness for a history that stretches back further into the life of the planet. We want more cousins so that, in the best sense, we can be better neighbors. We can acquire interior weight that will keep us rooted in our new homes. That is why we need to read these essays on the ethnic history of Minnesota. We need to meet those neighbors and listen to new stories.

We need also the concrete underpinning of facts that they provide to give real body to our tribal myths if those myths are not to drift off into nostalgic vapor. Svenskarnas Dag and Santa Lucia Day will not tell us much about the old Sweden that disgorged so many of its poor to Minnesota. At the height of the Vietnam War, an old schoolmate of mine steeled his courage to confess to his stern Swedish father that he was thinking both of conscientious objection and, if that didn't work, escape to Canada. He expected patriotic disdain, even contempt. Instead the upright old man wept and cried, "So soon again!" He had left Sweden early in the century to avoid the compulsory military draft but told that history to none of his children. The history of our arrival here does not lose its nobility by being filled with draft-dodging, tubercular lungs, head lice, poverty, failure. It gains humanity. We are all members of a very big club—and not an exclusive one.

I grew up in western Minnesota surrounded by accents: Icelandic, Norwegian, Swedish, Belgian, Dutch, German, Polish, French Canadian, Irish, even a Yankee or two, a French Jewish doctor, and a Japanese chicken sexer in Dr. Kerr's chicken hatchery. As a boy, I thought that a fair-sized family of nations. Some of those tribes have declined almost to extinction, and new immigrants have come to replace them: Mexican, Somali, Hmong, and Balkan. Relations are sometimes awkward as the old ethnicities bump their aging dispositions against the new, forgetting that their own grandparents spoke English strangely, dressed in odd clothes, and ate foods that astonished and sometimes repulsed their neighbors. History does not cease moving at the exact moment we begin to occupy it comfortably.

I've taught many Laotian students in my freshman English classes at Southwest State University in Marshall. I always assign papers on family history. For many children of the fourth generation, the real stories have evaporated, but for the Hmong, they are very much alive—escape followed by gunfire, swimming the Mekong, a childhood in Thai refugee camps. One student brought a piece of his mother's intricate embroidery to class and translated its symbolic storytelling language for his classmates. Those native-born children of farmers will now be haunted for life by the dark water of the Mekong. Ethnic history is alive and surprisingly well in Minnesota.

Meanwhile the passion for connection—thus a craving for a deeper history—has blossomed grandly in my generation and the new one in front of it. A Canadian professional genealogist at work at an immigrant genealogical center at Hofsos in north Iceland assures me, as fact, that genealogy has surpassed, in raw numbers, both stamp and coin collecting as a hobby. What will it next overtake? Baseball cards? Rock and roll 45 rpms? It's a sport with a future, and these essays on ethnic history are part of the evidence of its success.

I've even bought a little house in Hofsos, thirty miles south of the Arctic Circle where in the endless summer light I watch loads of immigrant descendants from Canada and the United States arrive clutching old brown-tone photos, yellowed letters in languages they don't read, the misspelled name of Grandpa's farm. They feed their information into computers and comb through heavy books, hoping to find the history lost when their ancestors simplified their names at Ellis Island or in Quebec. To be ethnic, somehow, is to be human. Neither can we escape it, nor should we want to. You cannot interest yourself in the lives of your neighbors if you don't take sufficient interest in your own.

Minnesotans often jokingly describe their ethnic backgrounds as "mongrel"—a little of this, a little of that, who knows what? But what a gift to be a mongrel! So many ethnicities and so little time in life to track them down! You will have to read many of these essays to find out who was up to what, when. We should also note that every one of us on this planet is a mongrel, thank God. The mongrel is the strongest and longest lived of dogs—and of humans, too. Only the dead are pure—and then, only in memory, never in fact. Mongrels do not kill each other to maintain the pure ideology of the tribe. They just go on mating, acquiring a richer ethnic history with every passing generation. So I commend this series to you. Let me introduce you to your neighbors. May you find pleasure and wisdom in their company.

Germans

IN MINNESOTA

Women of the St. Paul Turnverein formed a bucket-and-broom brigade, probably for a cleaning assault on the Turner Hall behind them, about 1920. Germans in many Minnesota communities formed Turner societies or Turnvereine for social and political activities and gymnastics.

O N A CRISP AUTUMN DAY in 1897, more than 10,000 Germans from throughout the nation gathered on the New Ulm bluffs to dedicate a grandiose monument to Hermann the Cherusker, the barbaric hero whose victory in 9 A.D. saved their Germanic ancestors from absorption into the Roman Empire. The statue, an American pendant to an even more grandiose Hermann erected 27 years earlier on the hills of northern Germany to celebrate victory over France and the creation of the German Empire, symbolized German American pride in their newly powerful fatherland. But it also affirmed their contribution as Germans to America.

"In Hermann and his deed are embodied not only German virtues, but the civic virtues of every high-minded person," proclaimed the keynote speaker at the monument's dedication. "Americans are a noble, industrious, progressive, public-spirited people, and we have become an integral part of that people." New Ulm itself, his audience knew, was chosen for this national monument because its stirring history and prosperous homes embodied the cultural ideals, toil, and courage with which Germans endowed their new homeland. But, he continued, "if, as citizens of this country we swear to it our steadfast loyalty, we still remember with love the country where . . . as children we romped on the playgrounds of merry youth. . . . Whoever is ashamed of the land of his birth, is also ashamed of his mother. And believe me, he will never become a good husband or father, never a good citizen of any other country." For America's sake as much as for their own, he urged on them a solemn oath. "Let us here, at the foot of the statue of Hermann, swear to maintain and exercise in this country everything good, faithful, noble, and true which adorns the German national character. May this monument proclaim to later generations that it was

New Ulm's 102 foot high Hermann monument in 1940. The statue by sculptor Alfonzo Pelzer of the W. H. Mullins Company of Salem, Ohio, stands atop a temple designed by one of New Ulm's original settlers, architect Julius Berndt, whose efforts brought the monument sponsored by the national Order of the Sons of Hermann to New Ulm.

erected by men who were loyal alike to the land of their birth and to the fatherland of their choosing."[1]

Hermann the German, as the statue has been known familiarly to generations of Minnesota schoolchildren, still brandishes his incongruous sword over the placid Minnesota River Valley, though time and desecration have taken their toll on copper, steel, and stone. But an even greater toll has been levied on the aspirations Hermann was meant to embody. Germans, Minnesota's largest immigrant group throughout the 19th century and still the state's largest ancestry group, are also one of its most invisible. Though the actual number of Minnesotans claiming German ancestry declined by more than 10% since 1990, more than 37% still claimed some German ancestry in the 2000 census, compared with not quite 29% for Norwegian, Swedish, and Danish combined. Yet Minnesota's image remains that of a Scandinavian state, while neighboring Wisconsin takes German honors with a German ancestry only five percentage points greater than Minnesota's. Three, four, and more generations and two World Wars away from their immigrant ancestors, most Minnesotans of German descent exhibit few obvious traces of ethnic distinctiveness. Despite the vows taken at the Hermann dedication, relatively little German is heard today in Minnesota, and most of the state's once ubiquitous German ethnic organizations have long since faded away. His German American sponsors, their membership in decline, were forced to turn Hermann himself over to the city of New Ulm in 1929. Absorption into American society, not ethnic persistence, became the German American story that New Ulm's statue tells.

But the story of Germans in Minnesota is more than the collective story of ethnic group identity, organization, and public influence. It is also the sum of hundreds of thousands of individual and family experiences, ongoing stories that did not end as the collective group story ran its course, but continues along paths marked by the experiences of earlier generations. Today many Minnesotans of German descent, like counterparts elsewhere in the nation, are seeking to recover some of their lost sense of ethnic identity. The Hermann statue is undergoing major restoration, and Congress in 2000 designated it a National Monument, recognizing German American achievements and contributions. But Minnesota also harbors numerous communities and families whose habits and values bear living witness to a heritage deeply rooted in a German past. The landscape and public culture of the state itself have been indelibly shaped by its German-stock citizens. This living cultural heritage is in no need of restoration. It just needs voice to tell its stories.

Numbers and Locations

It can be hard to pin down just who actually is German, since the shifting boundaries of Germany and the varied European homelands of German-speaking peoples preclude simple geographical identification. Only in 1871 did Prussia finally unite what in 1815 were thirty-eight small German states into a single nation whose boundaries changed three times more during the 20th century, and many German speakers always remained outside that nation. But specific national allegiances were often less significant for German immigrants than cultural commonalities. Shared settlements, associations, and newspapers created a kind of umbrella pan-German identity in America under which regional identities could also flourish. Thus, like the immigrants, we too should consider as Germans any of those people from a conglomerate of central European countries who spoke different but mutually intelligible German dialects and, if literate, read High German. At various times they have included people from not only modern Germany but also Luxembourg, the Alsace, parts of Switzerland and Poland, Austria, the rimland of Bohemia, local regions in Hungary, Yugoslavia, and other southeastern European countries, as well as the Black Sea and central Volga regions in European Russia.

But even if we simply consider as German those who identified themselves to American census-takers as born in "Germany" or in one of the states that later became part of the German Empire, the early and enduring German presence in Minnesota is clear. In the 1860 census, the first federal census taken after Minnesota became a state, some

16,000 persons, or about 9% of the new state's population, were reported as German born. Ten years later, perhaps every fifth Minnesotan was either German born or of German parentage, as was also the case in 1880 when census takers found 152,138 first- and second-generation Germans in Minnesota. At the turn of the century, when first-generation Germans alone numbered 116,973, they were still the leading single foreign-born group in the state. And even when foreign-born Germans dropped to second place behind the Swedes in 1905, they and their children and grandchildren nevertheless remained by far the largest foreign-stock group in the state, the position they have retained even as first-generation numbers continued their sharp decline throughout the 20th century.[2]

Germans are not only Minnesota's most numerous ancestry group, they are also, as the map of their 2000 distribution suggests, its most widely dispersed. The German presence is diluted only in the Twin Cities, the Swedish belt north of St. Paul, the Norwegian counties in the state's northwestern corner, and the Native American and mining regions of the north. But equally striking is their persisting concentration since the territorial period in four rural areas of the state: a great band south and west along the Minnesota River and dipping to the Iowa border, another along the Mississippi to the southeast centered on Winona, a third up the Mississippi to the north focused on Stearns and Morrison Counties, and a fourth in Minnesota's western "notch."

Why They Left Germany

What brought so many Germans to Minnesota to dominate so much of the state at so early a date? The simplest answer is that the opening of Minnesota to white settlement coincided with peak immigration years for Germans seeking farms and jobs in America. But a more satisfying

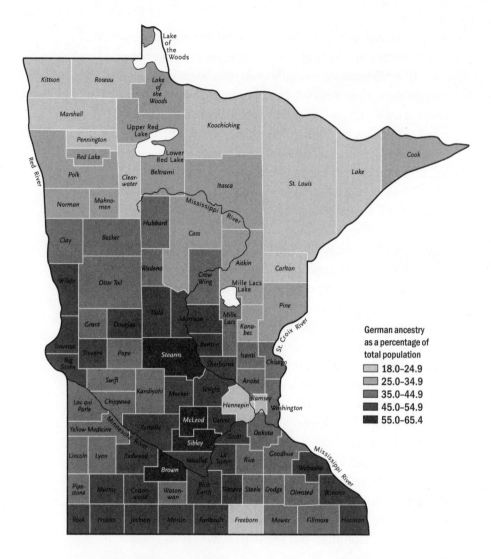

Areas of German settlement in Minnesota, according to percentage of county population reporting German ancestry in the U.S. Census of 2000

answer demands a broader perspective. Migration was always a component of life in even the most traditional of European societies. Local populations could easily outgrow their land. Famine, disease, or war offered one solution, marriage restrictions or intensified economic development were others. But another was always migration to areas where opportunity was greater, perhaps because disaster had devastated a local population, or conquest had opened new land, or new technologies brought previously unused land into production. Southwestern Germany, in particular, with its small-scale peasant agriculture, was historically a fertile recruiting ground for new settlers to populate developing areas of Europe. Thus it was no accident that Germans from this fragile, often war-torn region responded favorably to William Penn's invitation to help develop his new American colony in 1683. They inaugurated an overseas migration that by 1820 (when the United States government first began to collect immigration data) had brought an estimated 120,000 Germans to America. They settled particularly in Pennsylvania and New York and soon filtered westward into the Appalachians. Their productive, German-speaking farming communities harbored perhaps 10% of the American population at the time of the Revolutionary War.

Decades of war dammed the flow of migration from Germany after 1775, but with the return of peace to the Atlantic world after 1815, the trickle of emigration gradually increased to a flood by the mid-1840s, spreading from its southwestern origins north and east to engulf most of German-speaking Europe. There were limited opportunities for a rapidly growing population in the politically divided German states, whose traditional economies found it increasingly difficult to compete with the factories of industrializing Britain or the fertile fields of America. Not until Germany's postunification economic boom of the mid-1880s finally absorbed its surplus labor did the high tide of immigration begin to turn. Almost 5.6 million Germans found their way to the U.S. between 1820 and 1930, when U.S. immigration restriction and the Great Depression effectively ended the mass immigration. They formed the nation's single largest immigrant group to that time. Most were not the poorest of the poor, but peasants, laborers, rural artisans, even members of Germany's small middle class, people fleeing declining opportunity and often immigrating as families with capital and skills to invest, though single young job seekers became increasingly common as the 19th century wore on.

America's appeal for Germany's peasants and artisans was summarized in a letter that Friederich Schmitz wrote from Stillwater in 1858 to his parents in the Rhine Province. "Anyone in Germany, like myself, or most of those in our village, who marries and has a family can see in advance that he is to be and remain a poor and worried person as long as he lives. And in addition he must take his hat off to anyone who has a handful more of land, scraping and bending as the custom is. That is not done here. Any-

Third-generation German American artist Adolf Dehn, born in Waterville in 1895, captures in this 1927 lithograph of *Pommeranian Potato Diggers* the privation and degradation that led families like his to seek a better life in America. Dehn visited Pomeranian relatives while living in Europe after World War I.

one here who has nothing and is in health can support himself better than one in our village who may possibly have property to the amount of one thousand thaler. . . . And if one will work in this way for three or four years, he will be able to buy himself a small landed property."[3] This was a prospect with obvious appeal to the peasants of the German southwest, where generations of equal inheritance meant ever smaller plots of land on which to support a family, ever greater numbers of landless laborers, ever more small-town artisans and shopkeepers trying to make a living serving impoverished neighbors. In areas like Westphalia to the north, where viable farms were preserved by limiting inheritance to only one child, it appealed to landless children and to parents who saw that traditional pursuits like weaving could no longer provide livings to non-inheriting offspring in the face of factory competition. It appealed equally farther east, to peasants newly freed from serfdom, burdened by the costs of freedom and pressured by landlords seeking to rationalize labor on large estates.

The ranks of these economic migrants were leavened by groups of political refugees, particularly following the abortive 1830 and 1848 revolutions and again during Bismarck's crackdowns against socialists in the 1870s and 1880s—significant less for their numbers than for the educated leadership they provided and for the liberal, free-thinking religious and political views they cultivated. Refugees of a different kind were the Old Lutherans from northeastern Germany who beginning in 1839 fled state efforts to unite the Lutheran and Reformed (Calvinist) churches, the Roman Catholic clergy and nuns pressured by Bismarck's Kulturkampf in the 1870s, and the descendants of earlier German colonists in Russia who, by the 1870s, faced forced Russification and military service. Desire to avoid the military draft was an added incentive to emigrate for many in Germany as well.

There were formalities to legal emigration from the

various German states—debts to be cleared, fees to be paid, ties to be severed from all claims on assistance from local communities, military obligations to be fulfilled. Those who could not meet those stipulations fled "by night and fog," as the German saying went, emigrating secretly without papers and sometimes under assumed names. On the other hand, some local communities were so eager to free themselves of the burden of their poor that they paid the costs of emigration. Most emigrants, however, either paid their own way by liquidating their German property, using the surplus to get started in America, or their fares were paid by remittances sent by family members already in America.

As in the colonial period, much of the 19th century migration was a chain migration of family members, friends, and neighbors, who followed in the footsteps of earlier migrants whose letters and material assistance took some of the uncertainty out of the arduous move to the New World. There were occasionally also more formal colonization schemes, particularly in the 1830s and 1840s, the largest of which was the effort of a group of noblemen organized as the Adelsverein to settle several thousand impoverished immigrants in Texas beginning in 1843. Agents of shipping firms specializing in the emigrant trade provided information and passage arrangements. Antwerp, Rotterdam, and Le Havre were important ports of embarkation for southwestern Germans, but as northern and central Germany began sending more emigrants, Bremen and Hamburg emerged as Germany's leading emigrant ports. Early immigrants often took passage on ships heading for Philadelphia, Baltimore, or New Orleans to pick up wheat, tobacco, or cotton cargoes for the European market. As New York absorbed more and more of America's export trade, it became the main port of arrival for German immigrants as well. The trip by sailing ship usually took four to six weeks. By the later 1850s it was increasingly common, though more expensive, to travel by steamship, which shortened the journey to a predictable two weeks. As immigration intensified, transatlantic fares also declined.

Some German immigrants remained in the ports of arrival, either because they found opportunity there or because they lacked the funds to travel farther. But most moved inland as quickly as possible to find the cheap land, high wages, and business possibilities that awaited the enterprising closer to the settlement frontier. Routes westward from Philadelphia and Baltimore led to the Ohio River Valley, where a corridor of German settlement centered on Cincinnati by the 1820s. It soon intersected with another around

Opportunity in mid-19th century Germany was limited even for the well-educated sons of a Bremen merchant like future St. Paul bankers Gustav and Ferdinand Willius, shown here (left and center, with unknown boy) in 1847, about the time Ferdinand left school and six years before his emigration. Gustav followed him to America three years later.

St. Louis that emerged as Germans moved up the Mississippi from New Orleans. The third leg of the Midwest's "German Triangle" was formed when the 1825 opening of New York's Erie Canal brought Germans to the new towns and farmlands of the Great Lakes, and particularly to Wisconsin, which opened to white settlement just as German immigration intensified in the late 1830s. By 1850 almost half of America's German born resided in the Midwest. Some dispersed within the general population, but more congregated as laborers, shopkeepers, and artisans in the growing German neighborhoods of cities like Cincinnati, St. Louis, Milwaukee, and Chicago or colonized the countryside with farming communities often defined as much by religion as ethnicity.

Most of the colonial Germans were Protestant, since British authorities discouraged Catholic immigration, and Catholics in any case found a warmer welcome from Austrian and Russian authorities seeking to repopulate newly acquired regions in southeastern Europe. Despite the common association of southern and western Germany with Catholicism, and northern and eastern Germany with Protestantism, religious divisions actually formed a complex patchwork that left significant Protestant areas within Catholic Bavaria, for example, and found Protestant Prussia after 1815 governing not only the heavily Catholic Rhineland along Germany's western border but equally Catholic Westphalia to the north and Silesia far to the east. These accidents of religious geography meant that as many as two-fifths of antebellum German immigrants were probably of Catholic background, while Protestants from central and eastern Germany became more dominant thereafter. Early-settled Cincinnati became a center for German Catholicism, while Old Lutheran settlement in St. Louis and Milwaukee gave those cities a stronger Protestant stamp. Germans were welcomed in the new areas of the Midwest for their economic contributions, but their religious and cultural values—particularly their fondness for beer and public Sunday socializing—often antagonized reform-minded Americans. The early 1850s, in particular, were years of significant anti-immigrant agitation.

Why Minnesota?

These established German American settlements provided most of Minnesota's first German pioneers. Unlike new arrivals, Germans already in the U.S. were in a good position to learn about frontier opportunities, had the experience needed to survive in a chancy frontier environment, and often had strong motivation to move west. Perhaps they had joined earlier immigrants in a community already too developed to provide the land or jobs they were seeking, or as their children matured the same pressures that drove them to America in the first place drew them west once again. Or maybe they had simply learned, like other Americans, to see the frontier as a peculiar source of opportunity for those who got there first. Whatever the case, as Minnesota's shared world of Indians and fur traders slowly yielded to the forces of Euro-American development and acquired territorial status in 1849, Germans from farther south began filtering up the easily traveled Mississippi in response to its lure.

Eugen Gass has been identified as Minnesota's first German resident, an educated German-Swiss who emigrated to the U.S. in 1825 and twelve years later traveled to Fort Snelling from St. Louis seeking work. He was hired by Mendota fur trader Jean Baptiste Faribault to keep his books and teach his children and then worked a while for Henry Sibley before returning to St. Louis in 1840. There were also Germans among the soldiers keeping watch on the territory's frontier. By the fall of 1850, for example, the census taker counted 21 Germans among Fort Snelling's 143–man garrison, while 15 of the 54 soldiers stationed upriver at Fort Gaines (later Fort Ripley) were also German. Occasional Germans found jobs in the fur trade, including Peter Stein and his wife, who were trading with Indians in the Wabasha area that year, and young Christopher Highhouse and Michael Clossen who worked for fur traders up the Mississippi at Sauk Rapids. A German-speaking Catholic missionary stationed in Michigan, Father Francis Xavier Pierz, visited the French and Ojibwe of the Grand Portage area as early as 1838, and in the spring of 1852 founded a more lasting Minnesota mission at Crow Wing. In 1856 the Old Lutheran Missouri Synod sent Rev. Ferdinand Sievers from Frankenlust, Michigan, to explore

A Frontier Company Town

In 1848 a St. Louis sawmill owned by two German immigrants, Frederick Schulenburg and Adolphus Boeckeler, bought the first raft of pine logs sent down the Mississippi from Wisconsin pineries. Five years later Schulenburg came upriver to Stillwater to locate a sawmill for the firm closer to the pineries, and soon the Schulenburg and Boeckeler mill was the largest in the state. To attract and retain a qualified, largely German workforce, they laid out a company town on the paternalistic German model just north of Stillwater, complete with company store, boardinghouse, workers' houses, and even a brewery, all soon overlooked in familiar German fashion by Schulenburg's mansion on the bluffs above. "Dutchtown," as it came to be known, had about 50 houses by 1860; only five of the 89 adults in the community had been born in the United States. Germans still comprised 92 % of Dutchtown's residents in 1880, when the firm employed about 400 in its Stillwater yards and mill. The mill helped account for the early and lasting German presence in the Stillwater area, and its partners and employees played important roles in the city's civic life. But timber depletion, the death of the partners, and the Panic of 1893 proved too much for the firm, and today the main signs of its once-vital presence are Stillwater's still-evident German heritage and some of Dutchtown's little 19th-century houses.

The second Schulenburg-Boecker sawmill at Stillwater was built 1876 and burned down 1892. The company office, hotel, store, and barn are in the background, with Dutchtown houses in the trees behind and the owner's mansion, in good German style, on the bluff above.

mission possibilities and the following spring established a Crow Wing mission of its own.[4]

Territorial governance brought an important circle of Pennsylvania Germans to Minnesota in the train of Alexander Ramsey, Minnesota Territory's first governor, whose mother was Pennsylvania German and who spoke her dialect; the associates who followed him included future governor Stephen Miller, who settled in St. Cloud with his Swisshelm and Mitchell relatives. It was yet another kind of frontier opportunity that accounted for the territory's largest concentration of Germans at midcentury, however. The new pineries and sawmills of the St. Croix attracted job-hungry Germans from St. Louis and other downriver settlement areas. By 1850 Washington County's 55 German men included not only laborers and lumberjacks but also a few craftsmen, a couple of doctors, and nine farmers, most of them family men, harbingers of the colonization to come.[5]

The steamboats also brought German-born merchants and craftsmen to the new territory's trading entrepôt of St. Paul. Bartlett Presley—his name already indicates his Americanization—illustrates the pattern. St. Paul's first German businessman was born in Baden in 1823 and emigrated with his family to St. Louis as a teenager, where he worked in the grocery and fruit business. His search for the right opportunity took him upriver first to Quincy, Illinois, where he married, and then in 1849 to Galena. But his younger sister, Mary, had married a young St.

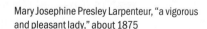

Mary Josephine Presley Larpenteur, "a vigorous and pleasant lady," about 1875

Louis businessman named Auguste Larpenteur, who moved to St. Paul in 1843 to work for a mercantile firm and was now preparing to go into business for himself. They invited the Presleys to join them in the infant city, and so later in 1849 Presley moved his family farther upriver to St. Paul, where he established a fruit and cigar business. "Short and chunky," representing "the German type of man, with heavy features and a slow and cautious movement," speaking "a little broken and somewhat thick" and always on the go, Presley later moved into fruit wholesaling, served three years as St. Paul alderman and six years as fire department chief, and at his death in 1884 was estimated to be worth $300,000.[6] Three carpenters, a couple of cabinetmakers, two stonemasons, a butcher, a cigarmaker, and a couple of laborers comprised the other German men found by the census taker in St. Paul in 1850; somehow Anthony Yoerg, who had arrived in St. Paul in 1848 and with his son established Minnesota's first brewery, escaped his notice. Only Presley, a carpenter from Illinois, and one of the laborers had families with them, as did two farmers on the town's edge, one from Missouri and the other from Pennsylvania. Nearby St. Anthony's mid-century German community was even smaller: one maid, five laborers, and John Orth, Minnesota's second pioneer brewer, an Alsatian recently arrived from Pennsylvania with his very pregnant wife.[7]

But Minnesota's greatest lure for German peasants was its land. When Minnesota became a territory in 1849, legal settlement was possible only in the triangle of land between the St. Croix and the Mississippi. A series of Indian treaties between 1851 and 1855 soon opened much of the future state to white settlement, and Germans were quick to take advantage of the new opportunity. Cheap government land was also available in north-central Wisconsin, western Iowa, and eastern Kansas and Nebraska, but scouts from older German communities who ranged the West to check out potential settlement sites reported several telling advantages for Minnesota. Above all, at a time when the first railroads were only tentatively stretching across the Mississippi, Minnesota had fertile land lying close to that mighty river and its navigable tributaries, promising easy access for settlers to its land and for their products to market. Another advantage was that, unlike the prairie of western Iowa, for example, much of Minnesota was wooded. Wood meant cheap fuel, fencing, and building materials, feed for free-ranging hogs and cattle, firewood and ashes (for soapmaking) for use and sale, and game, nuts, and berries to help sustain settlers through the early years as family labor slowly cleared the land. Nor, unlike Kansas and Nebraska in the 1850s, was Minnesota directly embroiled in the nation's growing clashes over slavery. And when the Homestead Act of 1862 offered 160 acres virtually free to settlers who worked their claims for five years, Minnesota would be the most accessible area with large amounts of federal land for claiming.

The news of land freed by Indian treaty attracted German-speaking squatters even before legal settlement was possible. The two Diethelm brothers and their young families, for example, left Switzerland's Schwyz Canton for New Orleans in the summer of 1851. Carl and his family spent the winter in Cairo, Illinois, where he worked as a carpenter to earn money for the rest of their journey, but Michael and his wife continued upriver to St. Paul. Hiking into the woods, he located a farmsite south of Lake Minnetonka and then returned to St. Paul for winter work. In the spring the two families reunited at the claim to build a joint cabin, clear fields, and plant their first crops. Soon Tobias Ottinger came crashing through the woods to settle near them, his belongings on a stone boat pulled by a yoke of oxen bought with several years' earnings as a peddler in Missouri and points south. The six Kessler children and their widowed mother also drifted into the area that spring. They had left Bavaria sometime in the late 1840s to join neighbors in Cincinnati, only to find that their friends had already left for Michigan. Reports from Michigan were not promising, however, so the Kesslers remained working in Cincinnati until they heard about the new Minnesota land. These Swiss and Bavarian squatters shared not only an eye for good land and willingness to endure frontier privation but also their Catholic religion and quickly attracted relatives and friends to the settlement they would name Victoria. Within a few years, all ten of Mrs. Carl Diethelm's brothers arrived from Switzerland, while the Kesslers were quickly joined by friends from Michigan and Cincinnati as well as from Bavaria. The first Catholic missionary visited the squatter settlement as early as 1852, and by 1857 the settlers formed a parish and built their own log church and school.[8]

Chain migrations like these, first from elsewhere in the

The Hodel family, who emigrated from Switzerland in 1869, built this log cabin near Albany, Stearns County, in 1871 and lived in it for 35 years.

Many of the early settlers who came to Beaver Bay left within a year or two to seek more fertile farmland in southern Minnesota. The Wieland family stayed until 1880, when they sold the 3,000 acres owned by the Wieland Lumber Company. Charles Alfred Zimmerman took this picture of the village about 1880.

U.S. and soon directly from Europe, help explain the rapid emergence and expansion of German settlement clusters even before Minnesota became a state. But more deliberate colonization also occurred. Sometimes business was involved, as when the five Wieland brothers, who emigrated from Wurttemberg in the late 1840s, transferred their tannery interests and 25 German-Swiss workers from Ohio's Maumee Valley to Beaver Bay on Lake Superior in 1856. More frequently, religion played the central role. For example, the Reverend Sievers during his 1856 missionary trip found clusters of German squatters scattered between the Minnesota River and Lake Minnetonka and at Maple Grove along the Mississippi north of St. Anthony Falls. Many were from Hanover's overgrazed Luneberg Heath and had come north from initial settlements near Chicago, particularly at Cooper's Grove. Siever's letters to *Der Lutheraner,* the Missouri Synod's journal, publicized these settlements in German Lutheran circles, as did similar reports when the first Lutheran pastor arrived the following year from Cooper's Grove. Johann Peters, a recent arrival from the Hamburg area, was one of those who followed from Illinois that autumn; the next spring his two daughters arrived by rail and riverboat, while their mother Katherine joined neighbors to make the entire eight-week trip to Green Isle in Sibley County on foot, using her covered wagon only for sleeping since she could not afford to lose any of the cattle she was herding for the family's homestead. Soon Old Lutherans from established settlements throughout the Midwest were on the move to Minnesota.[9]

Religious auspices were even more central to the German Catholic settlement of Stearns County. Recognizing that Winnebago (Ho-Chunk) cessions were soon to open the land south of his Crow Wing mission to white settlement, Father Pierz wrote to Cincinnati's German Catholic weekly, *Der Wahrheitsfreund,* in a letter published March 1, 1854, inviting "Germans who live in overpopulated cities and are becoming too anglicized in the employ of Americans and Protestants" to claim these new lands for themselves. "I do wish that the choicest pieces of land in this delightful Territory would become the property of thrifty Catholics who would make an earthly paradise of this Minnesota which Heaven has so richly blessed, and who would bear out the opinion that Germans prove to be the best farmers and the best Christians in America." He promised a haven where they could practice their faith free from the anti-Catholicism of older areas; "do not bring with you any freethinkers, red republicans, atheists or agitators," he warned. Within weeks of the publication of his letter, scouts from separate German Catholic settlements in northeastern and north-central Illinois, southwestern and northwestern Indiana, northeastern, north-central, and southern Ohio, western Pennsylvania, eastern Wisconsin, and central Missouri had converged on the Sauk River Valley, and fifty pioneering families huddled in crude Minnesota cabins that bitterly cold winter. As a result of Pierz's "facile pen," wrote Archbishop John Ireland many years later, "came crowds of settlers, sturdy sons of the Rheinland, Westphalia and Bavaria, until a new Germany rose in Stearns County."[10]

A promotional view of New Ulm in 1860, undoubtedly aimed at potential German settlers. Note the spacious plan, the emphasis on easy steamboat access, the windmill in the center background, and the romantic depictions of Native Americans framing the foreground. Few of these buildings survived the burning of the infant city in the Dakota War of 1862.

But in fact it was "red republicans" who promoted Minnesota's best known German colony, New Ulm. Ferdinand Beinhorn arrived from Brunswick in 1852 with plans to establish a German colony somewhere in the west and in August 1853 founded the Chicago Land Verein (Land Society) with fellow students of English at a Chicago evening school. Following a common model of the time, they planned a group settlement financed by membership dues. By April 1854 their Chicago membership stood at about 800, mainly workingmen anxious to leave a cholera-ridden city, and by June their scouts, having rejected possible sites in Michigan and Iowa, were prowling the Minnesota Valley, where they remained for the winter. Their reports led the society the following spring to choose the present New Ulm location for its scenery, timber, and waterpower potential. They pre-empted 16 quarter sections and staked out a town plat fronting the river in a grid pattern that left several squares open for public use. Each member was to be assigned 12 town lots and an additional nine (later changed to six) acres outside the village. But before any lots were legally assigned, Wilhelm Pfaender and two companions, representing a well-financed group of about 1,300 Turnverein members, arrived in St. Paul from Cincinnati looking for a site for "a German settlement [with] avoidance of speculation, [and with] educational opportunities for the children of liberals and freethinkers." The Turner movement, founded in Germany in 1817, combined gymnastics with nationalism, anticlericalism, and political liberalism and even socialism and had gained increasing prominence in German American communities with the arrival of the 1848 refugees. Recognizing their mutual interest in establishing a German town, the two groups merged as the German Land Association of Minnesota, which was incorporated a year later on March 4, 1857, and capitalized at $100,000. The dream of a cooperative socialist settlement died with the financial disarray and dissolution of the association in 1859, but the community itself thrived. Its 635 residents in 1860 included only two who were not German.[11]

After the Civil War, railroads and state government

both played increasingly important roles in luring Germans to Minnesota. As early as 1858, following a trip from New York to Pine County, a Silesian 48'er named Eduard Pelz published a popular book about Minnesota in Germany that included advice for immigrants by Hermann Trott, a land agent for the St. Paul and Pacific Railroad Company, and Daniel A. Robertson, a St. Paul newspaperman. After he returned to Germany in 1866, he published a translated pamphlet on the state, and four years later, when the Northern Pacific Railway intensified its campaign to attract settlers, he established a monthly journal, *Der Pfadfinder* (The Pathfinder). Issued in Gotha, it contained articles about both North and South America, but particularly about Minnesota, with advertisements for the Northern Pacific Railway. Pelz regularly answered inquiries from correspondents throughout Germany. Like many promoters of Minnesota, he defended its climate as healthful, described its location in the temperate zone as particularly suitable for Germans, and emphasized its location in the center of North America as advantageous—an argument that also appeared in pamphlets written by others. Albert Wolff, another 48'er and editor of one of St. Paul's first German newspapers, translated Minnesota's official emigration pamphlet into German in 1866 and served as a state commissioner of emigration from 1869 to 1871. As Minnesota's representative in Germany, he reported that in 1870 he spread information about the state among 57 emigrant boardinghouses and 23 ships' officers and also found a ready audience among 13,000 Prussian soldiers and a troop contingent from the Rhineland quartered in Bremen on the eve of the 1870 war with France. The Northern Pacific also advertised the Minnesota region through thousands of leaflets distributed by agents in southwestern and northeastern Germany.[12]

Perhaps the most distinctive group attracted by such efforts were Russian German Mennonites, whose emigration

The Gerhard Dicks family immigrated from Pordenau, South Russia, in 1875 and in 1884 built this typical early Mennonite homestead with lean-to, shed, and barn attached to the house. It was restored and moved to the site of Heritage House, Mountain Lake, about 1960.

was stimulated by the fortuitous arrival of the State Board of Immigration's pamphlet in 1871, just as their military service exemption was withdrawn by Russia. Scouts visited Minnesota the following year and again during a larger North American tour in 1873. Most of the immigrants chose land farther west, but William Seeger, secretary of the State Board of Immigration, personally convinced a small number to settle near Mountain Lake in Cottonwood and Watonwan Counties, where his son had business interests. Within seven years, the Mountain Lake colony numbered about 1,700 persons. There were also smaller Russian German settlements of Catholics and Lutherans in Sibley and McLeod Counties.[13]

Nevertheless, private correspondence and reports in German American and German newspapers undoubtedly remained the main stimuli to Minnesota's German peopling. Fewer newcomers arrived directly from Germany by the 1880s, but many still responded to invitations like the one sent by Hubert Neumann of Bird Island, Renville County, to relatives in Germany: "If you know a good boy who wants to do farm work and would like to come to America, send him to me. I'll give him fair wages, and if he doesn't want to stay with me, he'll be free to leave. There are several Germans here who always employ farmhands."[14] And Minnesota's growing cities proved increasingly attractive to new immigrants, to Germans from elsewhere in the U.S. seeking jobs or business opportunities, and to farmers' children from the Minnesota countryside. By 1905, the towns with the greatest proportions of German born were service centers in German areas like New Ulm (22.4%), Mankato (10.4%), Faribault (10.2%), and St. Cloud (9.7%), and early entrepôts like Winona (9.6%), Hastings (9.7%), and St. Paul (8%). New immigrants continued to gravitate to St. Paul's established German community and to its neighbors South St. Paul (18.7%) and West St. Paul (20.7%) while generally leaving Minneapolis (3.4%) and Duluth (2.9%) to other ethnic groups.[15]

Livelihoods and Communities

The search for economic opportunity that brought Germans to Minnesota also shaped the communities that they built. Farming long remained their most important occupation, distinguishing them from Germans in most other states; by 1880, 60% of Minnesota's employed German born were in farming, compared with only 28.4% nationwide. This percentage exceeded the state average (51.6%) but was close to that of the Swedes and Norwegians (59.9%). Some 18.6% of all Minnesota farmers in 1880 were German born; only Wisconsin's 26.6% was higher.[16]

The randomness of the initial land claim process

meant that farming settlements were often shared at first by persons of varying ethnicities and faiths. But as more Germans arrived in an area, outsiders were often willing to sell out and move on, leaving community institutions and culture in German control. Only three of the original 47 claimants in Norton Township in Winona County were German, for example, but by 1870 it was 73% German and overwhelmingly Prussian; by 1894 all the land in the township was owned by Germans.[17] In Stearns County, as early as 1860, 12 German Catholic parishes stretched in a 40–mile chain along the Sauk Valley, and German patronage had already shifted St. Cloud's business center from the Yankee to the German quarter. By 1880 there were 30 German parishes in the county, and Germans dominated a rural core of 18 townships, 11 of which were more than 90% German and none less than 80.[18] Brown County German settlement similarly expanded from its New Ulm core, acquiring in the process a large German-speaking Bohemian element, thanks to the promotional activity of New Ulm's Catholic pastor, Father Alexander Berghold, a native of Styria, Austria.[19]

When contiguous expansion was blocked by other groups, newcomers and the maturing children of older settlers leapfrogged to the next frontier. Only two of the five Unke siblings from Pommerania, for example, were able to establish their families permanently in the Maple Grove area, where they moved from Wisconsin during the Civil War. The others relocated their maturing children to the Dakota frontier in the early 1880s, and by the turn of the century members of the next generation farmed as far afield as Alberta and western Oregon.[20] Stearns County Germans early established daughter settlements at West Union in Todd County, Millerville in Douglas County, and Pierz in Morrison County, later flooded into North Dakota (where "Stearns County German" remains a recognized ethnicity today), and in 1905 negotiated with Canadian authorities to establish the St. Peter Colony in north-central Saskatchewan.[21] In the decades after the Civil War, land agents from throughout the country advertised widely in Minnesota German newspapers, and the children of Minnesota's German pioneers soon were to be found wherever new farming land was opened for development, from the wheat fields of Idaho to the orange groves of Florida. "Most of the settlers here have raised large families," Carl Mathias Klein of Millerville remembered in 1930; "our children wander away continually to many different places. Only few come in new, or return."[22]

The Michael Reisinger family (Gertrude, Matthew, Walburga, Theresia, Michael, and Mary), recent immigrants from Lower Bavaria, all worked together to bring in their first harvest near Collegeville, Stearns County, in August 1890.

Those who remained in Minnesota's German farming areas nurtured a distinctive and exceptionally enduring rural and small-town culture. To be sure, there was little direct carryover of specific agricultural practices from Germany to the virgin lands of Minnesota. Germans were glad to exchange the inefficiencies of cultivating scattered plots in open village fields for residence on their own 80, 120, or 160 acre farms, even if it meant foregoing the daily

St. Michael, Wright County, shown here around 1900, is typical of the numerous villages that grew up around the churches established by early German settlers in the Minnesota countryside.

sociability of village life. They learned to clear land American fashion, to grow new crops and use new tools and machinery; former farm laborers and tenants learned to manage their own farms and market their products. But traditional attitudes toward farming as a vocation proved more functional and tenacious. German American farmers had a reputation for being conservative and unspeculative, more ready to rely on family rather than hired labor and to invest in fine barns rather than grand houses, more oriented toward long-term persistence of the family on the farm than to short-term profits, and Minnesota's German farmers often lent credibility to the stereotype. The labor of all family members, female as well as male, children and adults, on and off the farm, ensured its survival, while the farm provided the family with a living and children with an inheritance. Like so many others, the Rhineland's Randolph M. Probstfield slowly developed the Clay County farm he pioneered in 1859 through his own arduous work and that of family members. He still cut his barley with a scythe in 1875 while his pregnant wife bound the sheaves, and his daughter was plowing behind a team of oxen by the time she was 16. Like others in the Red River Valley he rode the wheat boom to prosperity by 1880, but it was his cautious diversification into vegetables, fruits, and firewood that enabled him to survive the farm crisis of the 1890s.[23] Such caution, along with religious stress on the virtues of rural life, larger than average families, lower than average educational levels, and distinctive inheritance practices aimed at keeping farms in the family, helped ensure that today Minnesota's dwindling number of family farms are even more likely to be in German-descended hands than a century ago.[24]

German family and economic values often played similar roles for those who found their livelihoods in Minnesota's expanding nonagricultural sector. For the unskilled, there were always laborers' jobs building roads, railroads, and towns, cutting timber, hauling goods, and providing personal services. But these were never as important for Germans as for other groups like the Irish. It was manufacturing, along with trade, that became their most significant source of nonfarm employment, thanks to the high proportion of skilled craftsmen within the German immigration. German artisans and shopkeepers became prominent fixtures in many Minnesota towns, and Germans moved quickly into factory employment as well. Hotel, restaurant, and saloon keeping were also favored occupations. Red Wing's 1909 lineup of German businesses was typical: two clothing stores, two hardware stores, two jewelers, a plumber, one wholesale and six retail grocers, a photographer, two druggists, a lumber dealer, three cigar

A Stearns County Courtship

This is a loose translation of a story that the editor of the St. Cloud Nordstern *wove around advertising plugs in his December 18, 1876, issue. His gentle satire captures the flavor of rural German life and the customs that helped keep farms in the family.*

He had loved her for many years—that was surely no crime. She loved him in return—and that too can be excused, for he was a very nice young man of 23 who was already managing the farm for his father.

"Heinrich," said his father one morning, "I am old. I can't handle the farm work as well as I used to. I've also, God be thanked, set aside enough that I can spend the rest of my days with the old woman there"—here he grinned over at his wife sitting behind the stove—"without such tiring work. And so I thought," he continued, glancing at his wife as if he expected her agreement, "that you should take over the farm."

"Ja," interjected the old woman, "I don't want to spend the whole day on my feet any longer either. If he'll take over the farm, I have no objections, I'd be happy—but he should get married first."

Heinrich turned red all the way behind his ears.

"Now Heinrich," interjected his father, "you heard what your mother said. Do you think you've got enough courage to court a wife, hum?"

"Oh," said the old woman, "I don't think Heinrich will have any trouble there. Didn't I see how he smiled at Fat John's Katie the other day when we drove over to the big prairie for a Sunday visit?"

"You see, Heinrich," laughed the old man, "Your mother notices everything, you've got to be careful not to make eyes at anyone when she's around! Well, fun aside," he continued, his face now very serious, "if you mean to get married, as your mother says, then, God willing, you can take over the farm in the spring."

"That satisfies me," replied Heinrich, "and I think I can get everything straightened out with Katie too."

He stood up immediately, grabbed his new hat, and headed to the door.

"Stop, stop," blustered his father, "where are you off to so fast?"

"I'm going to drive right over to Katie's, and see what she has to say about this."

"It's not *that* pressing," said the old man, "but if that's the way it absolutely has to be, then drive—I'll talk to her father when I have the chance. But I tell you one thing, you've got to get married within a month, otherwise you'll still have to wait a few more years."

Heinrich left the room happy as a lark. He'd been sweet on Katie for some time, but he was always too shy to say anything to her. Today he'd do it. When he came into the barn, his brother John was busy cutting straw. "Heinrich, what's wrong with you?" he asked. "You look just like Christmas and Pentecost have both fallen on the same day!"

manufacturers, four meat markets, a cooper, two brewers, two blacksmiths, a pump maker, a marble and granite works, a boat maker, a variety store, a sand company, an undertaker, a furrier, three barbers, two harness makers, an upholsterer, two wagon and carriage makers, four

An early 20th-century Stearns County wedding: the Kropp wedding's elaborately decorated bridal carriage and procession, St. Cloud, April 29, 1912

"John, hitch up the browns, and use the silver-plated harness, and the new buggy, and ride with me to the big prairie!"

"Ja, what the devil, what's going on today then?" asked John, completely surprised; "is there going to be a spree tonight?"

"No, no spree, just a courting!"

"Oh," John drawled, "now the light dawns! Yes indeed, that Katie really is a fine young girl, and I think she should also make a good housewife!" In less than ten minutes the buggy awaited Heinrich, who had gone to his room to change into his Sunday clothes.

When they got to their destination, they put the buggy in the shed and went into the house. Katie's father was busy at the fanning mill cleaning his wheat. The girls put aside their work and shook hands with the young men. Heinrich inched his chair ever closer to Katie and made his offer in a few words. Katie answered happily, yes. Then he went into the next room where her parents were sitting, and soon walked out beaming with joy. A wedding day was quickly set, and they decided to drive into St. Cloud next Monday to shop for things for their new home.

We wish them much happiness and blessings for their coming marriage!

hotels, and eight saloons. And a shoe factory recently founded by German immigrant Charles H. Beckman that survives today as Red Wing Shoes.[25] Like their country cousins, German wives and daughters were also expected to contribute to the family economy when they lived in

Anna Heger and Celia Tauer worked as maids at the Silverson home in New Ulm around 1911. Domestic service, a common occupation for many German girls, was often an important introduction to middle-class life and a way station to homes of their own.

town, taking in boarders, working in the family shop, taking in sewing or laundry, doing domestic service—occupations that were all the more critical for women who were single, widowed, or deserted. Sweatshop and factory labor, clerking in stores and offices, and teaching soon joined the list.

Real entrepreneurial opportunity awaited Germans who were able to amass some capital in this fashion or who brought it to Minnesota with them. Some of the most notably successful were those who found their first market among their own countrymen, particularly the brewers who slaked the German thirst for beer. Minnesota's brewing industry began in 1849 when a Bavarian, Anthony Yoerg, turned to beer production after his St. Paul butcher shop failed. By 1860 the state had added another 13 breweries: four more in St. Paul, and one each in Stillwater, St. Anthony, Minneapolis, Faribault, Mankato, Rochester, St. Peter, St. Cloud, and New Ulm. This pattern of dispersal throughout the state's German areas, bypassing Swedish and Norwegian concentrations, continued after the Civil War, as the number of the state's breweries, virtually all German-owned, climbed to a peak of 132 in 1880. While new breweries continued to be founded until Prohibition, the most important trend was the increasing concentration of beer production in a few large breweries; already in 1878 the top ten breweries,

The brewery of A. Schwarzhoff in Brownsville, Houston County, was one of two breweries and about 50 businesses catering to farmers and lumbermen in the Mississippi River town in 1870.

seven of them in the Twin Cities, produced 42% of Minnesota's beer.[26] The most spectacularly successful of the brewers was St. Paul's Theodore Hamm, a peasant's son from Herbolzheim in Baden on the edge of the Black Forest, who arrived in the U.S. in 1853 at the age of 28. He worked briefly as a butcher in Buffalo and Chicago, then after his marriage brought his bride, Louise, to St. Paul in 1856. Here together they ran a boardinghouse on the levee and then a hotel and saloon and in 1864 took possession of one of St. Paul's pioneer breweries in repayment of a loan. This was the start of a family business that at Theodore's death in 1903 would be producing a million barrels of beer a year and was, at the time of its sale to Heublein in 1965, the eighth largest brewery in the nation.[27]

Settlers' needs for supplies, equipment, and processing provided another kind of opportunity for enterprising

Hamm's Brewery stood near the Daytons Bluff neighborhood in St. Paul. The five-story brew house (here decorated for its grand opening in 1894), shops, and stable covered a two-block area. The Hamm family mansion, designed by a German-born architect named Augustus F. Gauger, sits on a nearby bluff overlooking the family business.

Germans. Nicholas Lahr, for example, trained in Luxembourg as a blacksmith and learned to make plows that could break tough prairie soil while working at his trade in Aurora, Illinois, after immigrating as a 24-year-old in 1853 with $200 in gold coins given him by his mother. A year later, having learned English in night school, he established a primitive manufactory of his own in the infant settlement of St. Cloud where he developed a plow particularly adapted to area soils. He was able to retire by 1873 and ten years later moved to St. Paul where he managed his real estate and mortgage investments and oversaw the education of his six daughters, all reportedly proficient in music and painting but also, in good German tradition, "trained so as to be self supporting in case of emergency."[28] Similarly, cabinetmaker Carl H. Klemer, who emigrated from near Berlin to Watertown, Wisconsin, in 1848 and then took his family by oxcart to a Minnesota farm in 1857, moved into Faribault at the end of the Civil War to set up a carding mill to process wool from area sheep. By 1877 he decided to install looms and weave blankets, and the Faribault Woolen Mill was born. Like so many German-founded firms, it long remained in family hands, through the fifth generation until 2000.[29] Another example of the same pattern was a Saxon, Gottlieb Schmidt, who opened a harness-making shop in Mankato in 1859. It grew from government contracts during the Indian War and soon became the largest harness manufactory in the southern part of the state. Over time the business expanded into other

Office of the Faribault Woolen Mills in 1897

lines and lasted through the fourth generation until 1986.[30] Even Minnesota's most spectacularly successful German entrepreneur, Frederick Weyerhaeuser, who began as a mill hand in St. Louis, acquired his first sawmill in Rock Island, Illinois, after the Civil War and moved his rapidly expanding logging empire and his family to St. Paul in 1891, followed the familiar pattern of drawing successive generations into the family business.[31]

Minnesota's German communities also supported bankers, lawyers, doctors, and other professionals. St. Paul's first German banking house, operated for most of its history by Ferdinand and Gustav Willius, sons of a Bremen merchant, opened its doors in 1856 and was reorganized as the German-American Bank in 1873, when it claimed to be among the dozen or so largest banks in the country. Historian LaVern J. Ripley has counted at least 20 19th- and early 20th-century Minnesota banks that had "Ger-

Martha Willius Claussen, daughter of the pioneer banker Ferdinand Willius, and her husband Oscar Claussen (shown here with their children in 1901) melded American comfort with German domesticity in their Laurel Avenue home in St. Paul's prestigious Summit Avenue neighborhood. Oscar Claussen, an American-born, German-trained engineer, designed many Minnesota power plants and sewage systems and was consulting engineer for the well-known Hastings Spiral Bridge.

Representative of Minnesota's specialized German craftsmen, Koenigsberg-born John Strauss, Sr., learned a special process for tempering steel in Italy and came to St. Paul as a 26-year-old in 1883, establishing himself first as a locksmith and then a racing bike maker. In 1890 he applied his steel process to manufacturing ice skates. From his shop on 165 West Kellogg Street, Strauss (shown here in 1938 with assistants William Blochinger and John Strauss, Jr., and an unknown customer) supplied the elite of the skating world, from Sonja Henie to Shipstad and Johnson, with hand-made skates until his death in 1946.

man" in their title. And this does not include others like St. Cloud's still thriving Zapp National Bank (no longer locally owned), which had its roots in the financial services that long-time Stearns County Register of Deeds John Zapp from the Rhineland provided fellow Germans beginning in the early 1860s, nor indeed the American National Bank and the major bank holding company founded by Otto Bremer, who came as a 19-year-old to St. Paul from the Harz Mountains in 1886.[32] German lawyers like New Ulm's Daniel Shillock, with his legal education from Koenigsberg and Berlin, needed to learn American law and gain English mastery before they could hang out their Minnesota shingles.[33] But their talents, and those of German-trained doctors, engineers, architects, and musicians, were often in demand beyond as well as within the ethnic

Two Generations
of Businesswomen

Marie Dreis, daughter of a Cologne artist, immigrated with her parents to Chicago when she was 14 in 1850. Four years later the family moved to St. Paul, and in 1860 she married bookbinder Peter Giesen, a fellow immigrant. Both played active roles in the city's German musical and theatrical life, and in 1872 Marie turned her hobby into a business, Giesen's Costumers, that would last until 1960. This energetic bourgeois wife and mother of four children provided costumes for amateur theater and opera groups, masquerade balls and costume parties, pageants, parades (including the Winter Carnival after 1886), and more professional productions. What began as an important service to the city's German cultural vitality be-

Mary Dreis and Peter J. Giesen celebrated their golden wedding anniversary in St. Paul in 1910

came by the early 20th century the third-largest, mail-order costume house in the U.S., sending costumes all over the country. The Giesens lived a comfortable, sociable German-speaking life on fashionable Daytons Bluff and then after 1907 at 184 Summit, closer to the business on Franklin. In 1903 Marie, now 67, turned the business over to her youngest son, Martin, who married Olga Hilbert the following year. Olga, a buyer of notions and trimmings for Field Schlick and Company, a St. Paul department store, was the daughter of a civil engineer and like the Giesens was active in St. Paul's German cultural life. She soon took over her mother-in-law's central role in the costume business, leaving Martin to socialize with customers and handle the finances while she researched, designed, and managed the thousands of costumes themselves. Her only daughter, Louise, was born in 1915 when she was 35. Louise went into radio, not costumes, Martin died in 1943, and finally in 1960 Olga reluctantly sold Giesen's, only to die two months later. Elaborate costumes were no longer in the same demand, and this legendary St. Paul firm nurtured by two generations of strong-minded German-American businesswomen folded for good ten years later.

community, and they formed an important part of its leadership group.

Indeed, Mary Lethert Wingerd has argued that St. Paul's large German community was unusually well-integrated into the city's business class, owing perhaps to their early arrival and success in the city and the absence of a cohesive group of wealthy Yankee industrialists such as those who dominated Minneapolis across the river. Like other midwestern cities, St. Paul developed extensive German neighborhoods, first along the Upper Levee and then out West 7th, up Daytons Bluff, across the river in West St. Paul, and near the rail yards in Frogtown. Successful Germans often retained their ties to the churches, associations, and institutions of these vibrant ethnic enclaves even when they left their working-class and lower-class neighbors for loftier Summit Avenue heights. But business partnerships and social relationships with non-Germans were also frequent; by 1915 some 20% of the elite Town and Country Club members had German names (another 20% were Irish). St. Paul's small but significant group of German-speaking Jews were active participants both in German community life and in these cross-ethnic alliances. Thus Maurice Auerbach—described by one contemporary as "small physically, quiet, thoughtful, positive, quick, gentlemanly, busy"—who began as a clerk after arriving from Germany in 1857, in partnerships with leading Yankee businessmen became the largest dry goods wholesaler in the state and married the daughter of Senator Henry M. Rice.[34]

German integration into the city's business community helped facilitate what Wingerd has described as St. Paul's creative response to the challenge of Minneapolis growth. The city could not compete directly with its industrial twin, but it could promote an attractive business climate by using its intersecting religious and ethnic networks to broker civic solidarity and labor peace. Where the

Employees of Christopher Stahlmann's brewery in St. Paul, about 1870. St. Paul's predominantly German brewery workers unionized early, with support from brewers dependent upon working-class customers. Stahlmann, a Bavarian who immigrated in 1846, established his Cave Brewery on West 7th Street in 1855. It was acquired by the Jacob Schmidt Brewing Company in 1900.

Minneapolis Citizens Alliance used every means at its disposal to suppress labor unions, by the end of the 19th century the closed shop was becoming the St. Paul norm. Even before the Twin Cities' first major burst of labor agitation under the Knights of Labor in the mid-1880s, German cigar makers, coopers, brewery workers, stonecutters, carpenters, and others began union organizing, sometimes forming separate German-language locals. Nevertheless, Germans do not seem to have played so prominent a role in Minnesota union history as in many other parts of the nation, perhaps simply because they were less numerous within the working class than elsewhere or perhaps because the state attracted more than its share of rural conservatives and fewer of the radical industrial immigrants of the 1880s. Perhaps St. Paul's distinctive labor climate and the customary paternalism of many German employers are also part of the explanation. Whatever the case, individual Germans like Emil Reinecke, whose cigar maker's union issued the call to form the St. Paul Trades and Labor Assembly in 1882, or Ernest Riebe, whose cartoons helped rally Minnesota's radical Wobblies (Industrial Workers of the World) in the strife-torn years of the 1910s, may have found their place in the state's labor history, but that of the group as a whole remains indistinct.[35]

The Kuhles and Stock Cigar Company was one of several cigar factories in the Twin Cities in 1900. This firm also employed women, who sorted the tobacco leaves.

Churches and Schools

Thanks to the nature of its immigration, the church more than the union hall remained at the center of Minnesota's German community life. Even free-thinking New Ulm became by the end of the 19th century a Catholic stronghold overlooked by a Lutheran college on its bluffs. In contrast to more homogeneous groups like the Irish, Swedes, or

Norwegians, religion divided rather than united the Germans, yet religion also reinforced their German distinctiveness. The state's German Catholics, like their counterparts elsewhere, benefited from financial aid and personnel sent by European missionary societies as they struggled to establish familiar forms of worship within an Irish-dominated Catholic church and long maintained a parallel world of their own within Catholic Minnesota. They gained strength and autonomy from their concentrated settlement patterns, particularly in the central part of the state, where the St. Cloud diocese was set off from St. Paul in 1875 and committed to the care of a series of German-speaking bishops. Even in the state's other three dioceses (St. Paul, Duluth, and Winona), the willingness of bishops to turn the care of sometimes troublesome German parishes over to German religious orders encouraged a certain cultural independence.

At Pierz's request, St. Paul's Bishop Joseph Cretin in 1856 invited Bavarian Benedictines from St. Vincent Abbey in southwestern Pennsylvania (founded ten years earlier as the order's first American monastery) to provide spiritual care to German-speaking Catholics in his new diocese. Soon three priests and two lay brothers established a primitive log-cabin priory on donated St. Cloud land and began a ministry that before long extended not only to the German Catholics flooding into Stearns County but southward to Dakota County and into St. Paul, where in 1858 they took charge of Assumption parish, founded four years earlier for the city's German Catholics. When their St. Cloud land title proved defective, they moved in 1864 to 1,280 acres around Lake Sagatagan, four miles from St. Joseph. Here, steadily reinforced by new arrivals from Germany and recruits from German Minnesota, they built what would become St. John's Abbey and University, an educational center for Minnesota's German Catholic men and a training ground for German-speaking priests.[36] By

1892, Minnesota had 182 parishes and missions that were served by 150 German-speaking priests, 56 of them Benedictines (there were also eight Franciscans in Scott, Carver, and Wright Counties and five Jesuits in Mankato). Only 20 were American-born (including 13 Benedictines). Many of

St. John's Abbey stood out plainly on the Minnesota prairie in 1900.

the remainder were recent refugees from the Kulturkampf in Germany, who preached a conservative homeland Catholicism to increasingly second- and third-generation parishioners.[37] Not until after the turn of the century did German Americans begin training at the archdiocesan seminary in St. Paul in any numbers.[38]

Benedictine nuns also came to St. Cloud from Pennsylvania a year after the pioneer monks, opening the first German parochial school there and in 1863 moving their motherhouse to nearby St. Joseph, where in 1882 they founded the precursor of the College of St. Benedict as a boarding academy for girls.[39] By 1892 they were conducting schools in 23 Minnesota German parishes. German School Sisters of Notre Dame from Milwaukee staffed another 17, Franciscans from Milwaukee eight, Sisters of Christian Charity from Wilkes-Barre nine, and the Dominicans of Sinsinawa (a non-German order) one. Fourteen German parishes had parochial schools taught by male teachers, while four in Stearns County reported as their parish school a public school "in Catholic hands." That probably also describes the case in many of the remaining three-fifths of German parishes that lacked formal parochial schools.[40]

Germans were even more committed than the Irish to maintaining parish schools in which German could be taught alongside Catholic doctrine in accord with the belief that "language saves the faith." But when they con-

The intermediate class of St. Mary's School, Stillwater, in 1908, with their Benedictine teacher. St. Mary's German Catholic parish was founded in 1865, 12 years after the founding of Stillwater's Irish parish, St. Michael's. By 1892, there were 115 German families in St. Mary's parish and 80 children in the school.

trolled the local school district, they often saw little need for the expense of a separate parish school. Occasionally they hired nuns to teach in these district schools, but more often they preferred lay men specially trained in Catholic seminaries like St. John's or St. Francis in Milwaukee to act as teachers, organists, choir directors, and sextons, a familiar German pattern. Likewise imported from Germany was their preference for a lay board of trustees to manage parish finances. By the 1880s and 1890s such preferences increasingly brought German parishes into open conflict with priests and bishops wanting to centralize control in clerical hands and promote a uniform American Catholicism. State authorities also increasingly challenged religious use of public funds, but tenacious communities like Avon in Stearns County could find ways to preserve essentially mixed systems throughout the 20th century.[41]

A rich community and devotional life developed around their tall-steepled Gothic churches in both country hamlets and city neighborhoods. By the end of the 19th century Germans had six national parishes in St. Paul and three in Minneapolis. Each German parish had its array of age- and sex-segregated societies and sodalities, a choir, and often a band or even a shooting society. Feast days throughout the year, like Christmas, First Communion day, and Corpus Christi, were celebrated with elaborate pomp and processions. Periodic multiday missions by visiting preachers sparked religious renewal, annual fundraising fairs recalled the *Kirmes* festivals of homeland villages, and traditional shrines and pilgrimages took new root in Minnesota soil. A widely circulated Catholic newspaper, *Der Wanderer,* founded in St. Paul by the Benedictine pastor of Assumption in 1867 (and still published in English today), promoted a statewide sense of common interest, which solidified when ten parish mutual-benefit societies united in 1878 to form the German Roman Catholic Benevolent Association of Minnesota. It grew rapidly

A Corpus Christi altar, probably in Cold Spring, Stearns County, around 1915. The feast of Corpus Christi—
Frohnleichnam—in early June was celebrated in German Catholic parishes with a festive procession of
parishioners, choir, band, white-clad girls strewing flowers, altar boys, and priests to outdoor altars
specially decorated by parish families.

and soon provided not only insurance but a statewide
focus for lay activism, extending membership to women in
1898. Three hospitals, an orphanage, an old people's home,
and two Indian missions rounded out 19th century Minnesota Germans' separate institutional world.[42]

German Lutherans were as prominent but never as
unified a Minnesota presence as their Catholic compatri-
ots. They were not only divided from other Lutherans by
ethnicity, but among themselves by differences of doctrine, liturgy, governance, and custom, and unlike Catholics had no single institutional structure to direct growth

and allocate resources. Numerous Lutheran mission societies in German-speaking Europe competed to send money and missionaries to America, and numerous American synods, some more Americanized than others, vied for Lutheran immigrant allegiance. Lutheran particularism was

St. Paul's German Lutheran Church and School (Missouri Synod), Amboy, Blue Earth County, about 1915. The parochial school was so important to German Lutherans that schools were often organized even before churches were built.

especially extreme in Minnesota, owing to the rapidity of its German settlement, the variety of its migration streams, and the diversity of Lutheran traditions already in the region. While settlers struggled to call pastors from their former homes, missionaries followed immigrants into the state and competed for their allegiance.

As a result, within ten years of the founding of Minnesota's first German Lutheran congregation in 1855—St. Paul's Trinity Lutheran—there were five separate Lutheran synods striving to organize Minnesota parishes. Four were products of Old Lutheran confessionalism, including the

Students at Dr. Martin Luther College, New Ulm, in 1907. "I am quite busy all the time," wrote "E. R." on this postcard photo. The college, whose mission was to prepare teachers for Wisconsin Evangelical Lutheran Synod schools, became coeducational in 1920 and was reorganized as Martin Luther College in 1995.

particularly conservative Buffalo and Missouri Synods and less-rigid Wisconsin and Iowa ones, as well as a new Minnesota Synod founded in 1860 with support from Americanized Lutherans in the East. There were so few ministers to begin with that an effective division of territory occurred. Buffalo concentrated on its early Washington County core, Minnesota in growing cooperation with Wisconsin retained strongholds in the oldest German settlements along the Mississippi and lower Minnesota, and Iowa expanded cautiously in the south, while Missouri aggressively pursued German expansion northwestward with an efficient system of itinerant preachers that pushed it into the lead. In 1882 another German body with roots in the East, Ohio, entered the state, gaining ground mainly at Minnesota Synod expense. Three seminaries were soon established, Dr. Martin Luther College in New Ulm (Minnesota Synod, 1884), Luther Seminary in Afton (Ohio, 1885, moving to St. Paul in 1892), and Concordia in St. Paul (Missouri, 1893). By 1924, the Missouri Synod had 230 pastors in Minnesota compared with 178 for the other German-derived synods combined.[43]

Like many Catholics, with whom they shared a taste for

steepled Gothic churches, the conservative Lutheran majority clung to German language and culture as the best way to preserve religious orthodoxy from secular contamination and made comparable sacrifices to support parochial schools, often even before they erected a church. Sunday schools began to gain acceptance only in the 1920s. Community life, whether urban or rural, focused intensely

on the congregation, as members met to call pastors, debate theological issues and synodical membership (some remained independent or changed allegiance), donate labor, and manage school and church affairs. Country pastors and teachers often had the use of a farm for their support. Choirs served as quasi young people's social groups, while reading societies, brass bands, and Christian Aid Societies (organized to bypass "usurious" commercial insurance) provided other foci for community activities. Ladies'

Young America's St. John's Lutheran Church decorated for Christmas in 1914

Aid Societies and formal youth groups had to wait until after World War I in conservative parishes, but the great church festivals of Christmas, Easter, and Pentecost, annual school picnics, and mission festivals with neighboring parishes reinforced the inward-looking church-centered community.[44]

By contrast, religion was more apt to aid rather than hinder assimilation among Protestants with denominational kinship to English-speaking groups. German Reformed (Calvinist) and Evangelical (unionist) pastors followed immigrants into Minnesota, as did Baptists, while Iowa-based German Presbyterians also had some success evangelizing among Minnesota Germans from Reformed areas in Germany. German-speaking Methodists also stepped into the religious vacuum created by the speed of early German settlement, organizing their first churches at St. Paul (1851) and Woodbury (1853) and using camp meetings and itinerant preachers to attract converts, sometimes in the face of stiff local opposition. Since Methodism was unfamiliar among those from Germany and held temperance as a key tenet, conversion already meant a good step outside German tradition; close links with English-speaking Methodists further promoted Americanization. In 1885 Minnesota Methodism's German Conference had 67 churches; by 1924 it dissolved into its English-speaking counterpart.[45]

While there were still others who "want all church humbug banished," popular German strains of rationalism, free thought, and anticlericalism found relatively little traction within Minnesota's predominantly agrarian immigration, except among New Ulm Turners and some circles in St. Paul and St. Anthony.[46] Non-churchgoing parents who wished a German education for their children had the option of supporting private nonsectarian German schools, the first of which opened in New Ulm in 1857 and St. Paul in 1858. At least four others followed in St. Paul in the next two decades, including a German-English Academy in 1862, which gained public funding in 1866 once Germans were elected to the school board. Its success encouraged the Minnesota legislature in 1867 to approve German-language instruction in public schools, the university, and the normal school at St. Cloud.[47]

Expressions of Ethnicity

Lacking political freedom, 19th-century Germans compensated by cultivating private sociability, and their imported habits of association fostered the rapid development of German ethnic culture in America. No sooner was there a core group of Germans in St. Paul in 1852 than they formed themselves into a "German Reading and Educational Society" to "spread culture, progress, enlightenment, and freedom of thought" as the surest guarantor of "civil liberty." A Turner group, a singing society, an orchestra, a theatrical society, and the first German fraternal organization, the Druids, followed within the next few years. The Association sponsored the city's first German ball in January 1854, the first German Fourth of July parade and picnic in 1857, and by the end of 1859 opened the Atheneum on Exchange and Sherman as a central meeting place for the city's growing roster of German organizations and festivities. In 1857 St. Anthony Germans founded their first society, the Turnverein, whose California Street hall served as the local center for German associational life. New Ulm's Turner Hall, built in 1857 and rebuilt in 1866 after burning down during the 1862 Dakota War, performed a similar function. Even smaller communities like Stillwater, St. Cloud, or Red Wing quickly developed German debating clubs, singing and drama societies, bands, sharpshooters' leagues, and fraternals of their own, replicating the same round of meetings, balls, concerts, theatricals, and picnics that helped mold St. Paul's Germans into a community by the late 1850s. As early as 1860 Germans from throughout the state began gathering for annual singing, gymnastics, and other festivals. By 1890, St. Paul alone had a roster of German organizations a hundred strong.[48]

State and national singing festivals brought German singing societies together for annual socializing, competition, and celebration of German ethnic culture. Here, massed singing societies parade in Stillwater during the Ninth Minnesota Saengerfest in 1877.

Some associations, like the fraternals, served mutual benefit as well as social purposes, but others helped Germans satisfy cultural needs that English-speaking America could not meet and, in so doing, changed American culture itself. This was particularly true of music. "It is a mission of the Germans," St. Paul's *Wanderer* insisted in 1868, "to teach the Americans what good music is, what it means, and how it should be performed." An informal string quartet organized in St. Paul in 1858 grew into the St. Paul Musical Society (1863), the city's predominant orchestral group for the rest of the century. The forerunner of St. Paul's Schubert Club (1891) was the Ladies' Musicale organized by German women in 1882, and one of the Schubert

"Carneval"

Three decades before St. Paul's first Winter Carnival in 1886, Minnesota Germans were already celebrating Carneval or Fasching, Catholic Germany's traditional pre-Lenten celebration. Minnesota revelers fortified themselves against Lenten rigors with masquerade balls, fools' assemblies, and satirical parades that helped bind Germans together and drew amazed and amused attention from their fellow citizens. St. Paul's 1870 Carneval season, for example, climaxed with a Rose Monday "Burlesque Procession" of some 20 horse-drawn floats on runners that wound through the snowy downtown streets to the music of an extravagantly false-nosed band. One float satirized the proposed removal of the capitol from St. Paul to the Kandiyohi County wilderness with "an immense painting of the Capitol, drawn by two yoke of oxen." Tariff debates were skew-

St. Paul during the 1886 Winter Carnival. Brewer William Hamm, Sr., was the first King Borealis Rex.

ered by two floats: four nabobs luxuriating in a splendid sleigh labeled "High Tariffs in the East," followed by "a rough, coarse bob sled, with seedy, poverty stricken occupants, intended to represent high tariffs for the West." Carousers in two sleighs sending a well-filled whiskey jug back and forth by wire burlesqued the idea of a telegraph linking Africa and Australia. But the hit of the parade was the 20-by-40 foot platform crowded with "a collection of men and women about equally divided. The masculine portion was engaged in washing, ironing and tending babies, while the feminines were making speeches, and gesticulating very violently with one hand, while with the other they were holding their spectacles upon their sharp noses." They represented, of course, women's rights. That evening, Prince and Princess Carneval were joined at a grand masked ball by a motley crew of everything from grotesque giants and unsightly dwarfs to "harlequins full of fun and mischief," and "peasant girls pert and piquant." Everyone unmasked at midnight, and great was the consternation when some of "the most desperate flirtations proved to have been carried on between men and their own wives." Dancing continued to the wee small hours "when the great carnival ended, and the gay revelers quietly sought their homes."

Alma, Harry, Milda, and Erna Buetow of St. Paul dressed in a range of costumes on February 20, 1916, perhaps for a Fasching party.

The Danz Band under the direction of Frank Danz, Jr., and the Great Western Band directed by George Siebert, posed informally around 1890 at one of the outdoor park concerts that were a central part of German community life. Frank Danz, Sr., and George Siebert were brothers-in-law whose Twin Cities musical careers began in the 1870s.

Club's early musicians, Bavarian-born Emil Oberhoffer, went on to direct the Minneapolis glee club that evolved into the Minneapolis Symphony Orchestra in 1903. Oberhoffer became its first conductor, while some 50 of its instrumentalists came from the Danz Orchestra, the largest of the ubiquitous German bands and orchestras whose music filled the cities' turn-of-the-century concert halls, park pavilions, beer gardens, dance halls, and saloons.[49] Music was as omnipresent in Minnesota's German countryside. Town brass bands and singing societies formed even before the Civil War, and farmers' sons were soon earning pocket money playing fiddle and accordion at weddings, house parties, and dances sponsored by local clubs and saloons. The oompah "Dutchman" sound that emerged from the German-Bohemian family bands of the New Ulm area in the early 20th century is an enduring ethnic contribution to American music. But love of music also ushered America's emerging popular culture into German communities. Young German Americans in St. Cloud during the Gay Nineties, for example, organized a Concert Mandolin Band, put on blackface comedies, and even mounted a marching band on new-fangled bicycles! Music also received emphasis in German Lutheran and Catholic churches with their shared traditions of teacher-organists and well-trained choirs, and St. John's became one of the main American centers through which the 19th-century Caecilian movement to restore Gregorian chant, and then in the 1920s the Liturgical Movement, entered American Catholicism.[50]

Germans as such had little early impact on the visual

The New Ulm Post Office, now the Brown County Museum, built in 1909, was designed in the Flemish Revival style, reflecting early 20th-century New Ulm's self-conscious celebration of its Germanic roots.

arts in Minnesota, beyond the important role in church decoration of painters like New Ulm's Anton Gag, a German Bohemian, or wood carvers like Collegeville Civil War veteran Peter Eich.[51] They left a more obvious architectural mark; both the state's numerous German Gothic churches and the self-consciously "Germanic" architecture of breweries and late 19th-century New Ulm homes are hard to miss. But Germans also introduced less obvious vernacular elements into Minnesota's domestic landscape, particularly where they could afford to replace log cabins before gaining familiarity with standardized American styles. Luxembourgers in Rollingstone built thick-walled

Wendelin and Julianna Grimm, who emigrated with their three children from Kuelsheim, Baden, in 1857, built this house on their 160-acre farm in Victoria, Carver County, around 1875; it is one of about 75 remaining Carver County farmhouses in the Chaska Brick style. Grimm brought from Baden a small chest of what he called "everlasting clover," and through careful selection of the most winter-hardy seed each year, he developed a strain of alfalfa that made northern dairy farming possible. His recently restored house is on the National Register of Historic Places and is the centerpiece of the Hennepin Parks Carver Park Reserve.

stone houses in the old country
fashion, while Germans in Carver and Stearns Counties often
built in a warm cream-colored
brick that looked like stone. Germans might adopt the temple-
and-wing shape of the midwestern farmhouse, but inside they
retained the traditional continental three-room *küche-stube-
kammer* (kitchen, heated living
space, bedchamber) arrangement,
with interior chimneys and the
kitchen dominant. High bank
barns with earthen ramps to the
hayloft and a flock of outbuild-
ings like smokehouses, spring-
houses, and summer kitchens
usually signaled a German farm.
Germans also built a number of
Dutch-type windmills in the
state; one, the stone mill erected
by Louis Seppman west of Mankato in 1862, stands today in
Minneopa State Park.[52] Germans'
romantic delight in nature and

One of New Ulm's early windmills, which during the
Dakota War of 1862 provided sniper cover for about
20 members of the Le Sueur Tigers militia who helped
hold off the attack on New Ulm's business district
about three blocks west.

outdoor socializing gave Minnesota not only numerous
beer-gardens that later fell victim to Prohibition but also
an early pressure group for public parks.

A lively German press gave more explicit expression to
ethnic concerns and helped bind the group, despite real in-
ternal differences, within a broader imagined community
of German America. At least 100 German-language newspapers, many of them short-lived, were founded in Minnesota in the century after 1855, more than 20 of them in
St. Paul alone. Twenty-six Minnesota communities at one

Cultivating Minnesota's Garden

It was no accident that Germans have made significant contributions to the cultivation of Minnesota's environment. Dresden-born botanist Carl Andreas Geyer surveyed Minnesota flora as part of Joseph Nicollet's mapping expedition for the U.S. Corps of Engineers in 1838 and 1839. Christian Prignitz's 1858 New Ulm plat was exceptional in the land it set aside for parks. William Buckendorf, a gardener brought from Germany by Dr. Alfred E. Ames of Minneapolis in 1857, became a pioneer florist and greenhouse operator, the first of numerous Minnesota Germans in the business, including the Bachman family, who began as truck farmers in South Minneapolis in 1885 and gradually moved into flowers in the 1920s. Dietrich Lange, a Hanover-raised Twin Cities educator and nature author, was president of the Minnesota Forestry Association and first president of the Minnesota Izaak Walton League (1922).

St. Paul's Como Park, part of the park system laid out for the city by landscape architect Horace W. S. Cleveland, was largely designed by Frederick Nussbaumer, a German whom Cleveland enticed to St. Paul from London's Royal Botanic Gardens around 1887. Nussbaumer, superintendent of parks from 1892 to 1922, nursed the neglected land around Como Lake into a beautifully flowered park; the 1894 "Gates Ajar," still planted today, and the 1915 Como Conservatory, are parts of his heritage. Dr. Justus Ohage, a Hannover-born Civil War veteran who performed the first successful gall bladder operation in the U.S. at St. Joseph's Hospital in St. Paul in 1886, also left the city an environmental heritage: Harriet Island. Ohage, commissioner of health from 1899 to 1907, tried unsuccessfully to convince the city that a park on the island, already much used by Germans for recreation, would benefit workers' health. So in 1900 he mortgaged his home to purchase the site and donate it to the city with the stipulation that "it should be conducted solely as a place of wholesome recreation, free of money-making amusement features."

Minneapolis parks also owed their formative development to a European-trained gardener, Swiss-born Theodore Wirth, superintendent of parks from 1905 to 1935, who also saw parks not just as places of restful beauty but as sites for active recreation as well. Hennepin County's Noerenberg Gardens also have a very German origin. Frederick Noerenberg arrived from Ger-

time or another supported a German-language newspaper. Often, like their English counterparts at the time, they had political party affiliations and combined local and national news with extra efforts to cover Europe and slanted their editorial emphasis toward ethnic concerns. Others were religious or more specialized, like the weekly humor paper, *Der Lustige Bruder* (Jolly Fellow), founded in Minneapolis in 1890 and published for 17 years.

The first three German newspapers appeared in St. Paul in 1855, reflecting both the city's growing German community and the willingness of political parties to support a German newspaper as statehood loomed. One of these,

Members of the Sunbeam Band, wearing homemade gingham bathing suits, enjoyed playing in the water at Harriet Island under the watchful eye of Mrs. A. E. Clark, who had organized the event for children from poor families in 1900.

many as a 15-year-old in 1860 and went on to make a Minneapolis brewing fortune (Grain Belt Beer). In the 1890s he began carefully developing his Lake Minnetonka estate into a model landscape of lawns, flower beds, trees, and a working farm, with plant materials the family collected from around the world. His daughter left the estate and its gardens to Hennepin County Parks in 1972. St. Cloud's well-known Munsinger Gardens along the Mississippi, developed in the 1930s with local materials and WPA labor, also reflect the German heritage of the city's first park superintendent, Joseph Munsinger, for whom they are named.

the Minnesota *Deutsche Zeitung* (German Times) was edited and published by Albert Wolff and Friedrich Orthwein. Two years later Orthwein established the *Minnesota National-Demokrat* as a Democratic weekly, while the *Deutsche Zeitung* became the *Minnesota Staatszeitung* (briefly edited by freethinker Samuel Ludvigh) and then as a result of mergers in 1877 the daily *Volkszeitung*, long edited by Wolff as a Republican paper, which lasted until 1941. New Ulm's 1858 Turner newspaper, the *Neu Ulm Pionier*, continued after the Dakota War as the *New Ulm Post* and survived until 1933; eight other papers also appeared there at one time or another. Minneapolis also produced

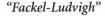
ten German newspapers over the years, the most important of which, the *Freie Presse-Herold,* appeared from 1869 to 1924. Winona had a particularly distinctive press history owing to Bavarian-born Joseph Leicht, a St. Louis newspaperman who moved to Fountain City, Wisconsin, across the Mississippi from Winona in 1869, established the *Westlicher Herald* (Western Herald, 1881–1924), and gradually built a German-language newspaper chain (National Weeklies, Inc.) through a series of consolidations with 22 German newspapers in Wisconsin, ten in Minnesota, and others in Nebraska, Montana, and Pennsylvania. German

As pioneer hardships faded, the genteel habits of Germany's middle class took new root in German Minnesota. Here, New Ulm women enjoy an al fresco kaffee klatsch around 1875.

Minnesotans also, of course, subscribed to many German-language journals published out of state. As new immigration declined and American-born generations increased, readership for Minnesota's German-language press waned; at least 20 German-language journals folded during the 1890s and the first decade of the 20th century, and by World War I, Minnesota had only one German-language daily and 18 weeklies in circulation.[53]

But cultivating the arts of sociability—*Gemütlichkeit*—remained the core expression of German American ethnicity. In parlors and backyards, saloons and clubhouses, church halls and picnic groves, Germans nurtured a public and private culture of family, food, fellowship, and festivity to heighten the sober round of American life. If Germans too often equated it with the beer whose consumption eased sociability, it nevertheless helped open Minnesota life to modern forms of public relaxation and was the main cultural expression that Minnesota Germans would unite to defend.

In the Public Sphere

Unlike Minnesota's Scandinavians, or the Irish in St. Paul, Germans were never able to translate their numbers, early arrival, and associational habits into group political power. No other German Americans followed Alexander Ramsey and Stephen Miller into the governor's chair, and only after ethnicity faded as a factor did Minnesota send half-

German conviviality moved outdoors in the summertime. The summer pavilion of the Tivoli Concert Hall at Wabasha and Bench was a "favorite summer evening resort" of St. Paul Germans in 1888, thanks to its "superb outlooks" up and down the Mississippi, its rich assortment of food and drink, and its excellent orchestra. It even offered a sheltered section "reserved for ladies."

German Democrat Eugene McCarthy to the Senate in 1958 and Republicans David Durenberger and Berlin-born Rudy Boschwitz in 1978. The list of German American congressmen until the later 20th century was almost as short. Democrat Henry Poehler, a Henderson merchant from Lippe-Detmold, served one term in 1878. Andrew Kiefer, a Republican businessmen and future St. Paul mayor born in Hesse-Darmstadt, served two terms beginning in 1892. Oscar Keller represented St. Paul as a pro-labor Republican for eight years beginning in 1919, and Westphalia-born Henry M. Arens, a Jordan farm activist, was elected as a Farmer-Laborite in 1933. Germans were politically engaged from the beginning, serving in Minnesota's territorial assembly and its constitutional convention. Indeed, a Luxembourg-born, Milwaukee-trained New Ulm lawyer, Democrat Franz Baasen, was Minnesota's first secretary of state. But the group was too divided by religion, class, and cultural values to form a reliable voting block capable of exerting statewide political influence.[54]

Most early Germans arrived in Minnesota as committed Democrats, thanks to that party's defense of immigrant and Catholic rights. By the late 1850s the new anti-slavery Republican Party proved increasingly attractive to freethinking and urban Germans, but many rural Germans remained suspicious of its nativist and temperance tendencies. Germans—a good seventh of the electorate—were courted by both parties in the critical 1860 election. The majority, according to Hildegard Binder Johnson, probably gave their votes to Lincoln and the Republicans.[55] But the Democrats retained heavily German Catholic Scott and Stearns Counties, and the Civil War years only intensified the alienation of Catholics and many Lutherans from the state's Republican government.

Many Germans, to be sure, were as eager to enlist in the Union army as any of their neighbors. Germans, about 14.7% of the state's adult male population, made up at

Private Fridelen Boll (1838-1917) of Company G proudly wears the regimental badge of the First Minnesota Regiment. Born in Freiberg, he came to America with his parents as a ten-year-old and was farming in Owatonna when he enlisted in 1861. He was discharged on May 5, 1864, and returned home to marry, father six children, and live out his life in Owatonna.

least 12.6% of Minnesota's famed First Regiment; some 20 Germans died at Gettysburg.[56] Indeed, by one estimate, Germans comprised almost 17% of all the state's Civil War soldiers.[57] But the great majority of German enlistments came after the first year of the war, under the threat of conscription or as a result of it. For every German who rushed to enlist, like Mexican War veteran Christian Bitka (a Nininger farm laborer who served in the First Minnesota) or Swiss-born St. Joseph farmer Friedrich Schilplin (who broke parole to join the 82nd Illinois and get back in the fighting after his Third Minnesota Regiment surrendered and who finished the war a lieutenant in the 113th U.S. Colored Infantry), there were others like 40-year-old Nicholas Friedman (or Freedman), drafted from his Stearns County farm into the Second Minnesota in spring 1864, who left a widow and four little children when he died five months later during the battle for Atlanta.[58] Many German newcomers felt little stake in the war and worried about families left exposed on the frontier. Such fears seemed justified when New Ulm was twice attacked during the 1862 Dakota War, and Minnesota Valley Germans bore the brunt of white casualties. When the same government that provoked the Indians and failed to protect German settlers from Indian wrath then drafted their menfolk and raided their cabins to round up resisters, little wonder that persisting resentment helped keep Germans divided.[59]

For most of the next forty years Republicans, in a nod to ethnic stereotypes of fiscal caution, kept German loyalists happy by slating Germans as state treasurer, while German Catholics and many Lutherans, particularly in the countryside, remained powerless Democrats in an effectively one-party Republican state. But what mattered more to Germans was control of local governments that affected daily life, and here they were far more successful. When Berlin (later St. Augusta) Township in Stearns County was organized in 1859, for example, Yankees were elected as constables and justices of the peace, but two of the three supervisors, the town clerk, the collector of taxes, the assessor, and one of the two overseers of the poor were all German; within two years there was seldom more than one Yankee holding a town office. By the early 1860s Germans generally controlled the Stearns County board and the offices of county treasurer, register of deeds, auditor, sheriff, coroner, and soon also school superintendent and judge of probate court. As St.

A Civil War Soldier's Wife Writes to Adjutant General Oscar Malmros

A few brief, well-written German lines (here translated) to German-born Adjutant General Oscar Malmros make clear the hardships of the Civil War for those left behind in the log cabins of the Minnesota frontier. William and Jette Krumrey were living in Scott County when the war broke out. He was 37 years old when he enlisted on October 25, 1862, in the Eighth Minnesota Regiment, Company I. The Eighth saw service in the Dakota War of 1862 and maintained a small garrison at Fort Ripley in 1863–64. Krumrey was discharged for disability on February 13, 1865. Perhaps his wife's pleas had some effect.

Big Woods
5 October 64

Honored Sir!

You will forgive a woman's boldness in burdening you with a request and I hope that your benevolence will not let it go unfulfilled.

My husband William Krumrey who is at present with the Reserve Veteran Corps at Fort Ripley has not had a furlough since March 1864 and all efforts to get one have been in vain.

I have been sickly since spring and the house—if it deserves that name—that I live in with our five little children is close to collapsing, during the winter it will soon fall down from cold and snow. That is why I am turning to you, believing that your intercession will soon permit the helping hand of my husband to reach us.

Respectfully
Jette Krumrey

Cloud's new German newspaper commented in 1876, "the Germans of the county should never underestimate the advantage of having a fellow countryman as county assessor."[60] At the state level, Germans could unite temporarily if their honor as citizens, German-language instruction in the schools, or their "personal liberty" to consume alcoholic beverages was attacked. As long as political parties kept those issues off the table, they could effectively ignore the German vote.

By the end of the 19th century, this became harder to do because agrarian insurgency weakened party loyalties and pressure for prohibition and English-only instruction mounted among reform-minded Progressive Republicans. Progressives numbered German brewers prominently among the "plunderbund" from whom they sought to rescue the state. Many Germans endorsed Progressive programs for government efficiency, business regulation, workmen's compensation, and electoral reform but were deeply suspicious of woman suffrage and drew the line sharply at county option for liquor sales. Yet even the rising threats to "personal liberty" were insufficient to overcome German mutual suspicions, and Catholics remained prominently outside the Minnesota branch of the German-American Alliance (founded in 1902 to oppose antisaloon forces), boycotting its 1909 German Day celebration in St. Paul and founding their own Catholic City Federation instead.[61] Effective unity came only after 1914, when the Alliance led other Minnesota German organizations and the state's German-language press in crusading for American neutrality in Europe's war and raising money for the German and Austro-Hungarian Red Cross. To critics who termed such efforts unpatriotic "hyphenism," the *New Ulm Review* replied simply that German Americans were "American citizens of German blood, who are first for their country, America, but have a very great sympathy (and it is right that they should have it) for the Fatherland."[62]

Looking for Disloyalty

N. E. K., an investigator for the Minnesota Commission of Public Safety, turned in his typewritten report datelined St. Paul, May 31, 1917:

At 8:20 a m I reported to Supt. C. R. H. who gave me full instructions relative to investigating conditions as to the [draft] registration on June 5th, also as to the pro-German feeling at St. Bonifacius [southwest Hennepin County] . . .

At 1:30 p m I left for St. Bonifacius, where I arrived at 6:10 p m. After securing a room at the hotel, I walked about town and visited two saloons, remaining in each place about an hour. Several men were playing cards in Cuyer's saloon and I entered into conversation with those who were talking German, but throughout the evening I did not hear a word spoken regarding the registration or war that could be construed as radical.

None of the men I talked with showed any indications of being radically pro-German or against drafting. 95% of the population in St. Bonifacius is German, although several different dialects are spoken, all of which I understood, and there were no pro-German or socialist demonstrations of any kind going on.

The townspeople in general seem patriotic as I noticed the greater number of homes have the American flag displayed in the windows and over porches, and as far as any talk is concerned, I could not find any indications that there was a radical element around. Signs were hanging in the saloons which read: 'War talk strictly forbidden here.'

At 10:30 p.m. I went to the hotel and discontinued.

They paid a real price for that sympathy when the U.S. entered the war on the side of Germany's enemies on April 6, 1917—though not, perhaps, as great a price as later legend would sometimes have it. Shakopee's Julius A. Coller probably spoke for most Minnesota Germans when he proclaimed at an autumn New Ulm rally that "the call of blood, strong though it may be, sinks into insignificance when there comes the call of my own, my native land."[63] But other Minnesotans had their doubts, and ten days after American entry into the war, the legislature established the Minnesota Commission of Public Safety with sweeping powers to enforce loyalty and aid the war effort. Germans were the most obvious target though its Twin Cities business backers used the Commission primarily as a weapon against the rising agrarian and labor agitation of the Nonpartisan League and the International Workers of the World. The Commission subjected Minnesotans to spies and denunciations, press and textbook censorship, registration of aliens, and intense pressure to enlist and to purchase Liberty Bonds. Some 56% of the 1,739 denunciations made to the commission in 1917 and 1918 concerned Germans. New Ulm's city attorney, Albert Pfaender, son of the city founder, and its mayor, Louis A. Fritsche, were removed from office for challenging the constitutionality of the draft, while Adolph Ackermann, president of Dr. Martin Luther College in New Ulm, was forced to resign under pressure for the same reason. Wisconsin-born political science professor William A. Schaper was dismissed by the University of Minnesota Board of Regents as a "rabid pro-German." A 60-year-old Red Wing miller, John C. Seebach, was sentenced to 18 months in Leavenworth for saying that the war was a "rich man's war" that the Germans would win because of superior men and resources. But it was betrayals from neighbors that Minnesota Germans would particularly remember: grand jury indictments for unpatriotic speech, yellow paint on barn doors, malicious damage to crops, demands that teachers and pastors resign, boycotts of German-owned stores.[64]

But local authorities in areas where Germans were numerous could shield their communities from the worst pressures as long as the draft and war bond drives proceeded smoothly. *St. Paul Pioneer Press* editor Bernhard Ritter, previously with the New York *Staatszeitung*, gave German Americans a sympathetic forum. Minnesota, unlike some states, never banned the public use of German or its teaching in schools. Only four of the state's 19 remaining German newspapers ceased publication during the war. Before the war, nearly two-thirds of Minnesota parochial schools used German, as did many one-room district schools in heavily German areas. War-influenced actions, such as Bishop Joseph F. Busch's early 1917 order that St. Cloud diocese parishes have at least one English sermon every Sunday, certainly hastened the slow generational

On April Fool's Day, 1918, the prominent statue of Germania, symbol of German pride, was removed from St. Paul's Germania Life Insurance Building on 4th and Minnesota. The Germania Life Insurance Company was founded in New York in 1860 and soon opened agencies nationwide. During World War I the company changed its name to the Guardian Life Insurance Company of America.

A speaker used a tank for his platform as he addressed a patriotic rally at Albany, Stearns County, during World War I. Every town and hamlet in the county organized Loyalty Clubs to ensure that war bond quotas were met.

process of language transition. By 1931 only 15 Missouri Synod congregations in the state still used German exclusively, but 13 congregations retained some German services as late as 1975. More than 90% of the families in one Stearns County township spoke German in the home in 1925; a quarter-century later, only 38% used no German at all. The 1940 census made clear that third-generation Germans were more apt to speak their ancestral tongue than was the case for almost any other group in the state; as late as 1980, 55,000 Minnesotans reported that they spoke some German at home.[65] German sociability also suffered when the collapse of the German-American lobby eased the passage of the Eighteenth Amendment in 1919 making wartime prohibition permanent, and many Germans interpreted woman suffrage in 1920 as a similar cultural blow. But the war paradoxically also encouraged renewed ethnic awareness in response to rejection as Americans, nowhere more evident than in voting patterns. Many German Democrats abandoned the party that had led the country into war, throwing support to the Nonpartisan League and then to the new postwar Farmer-Labor Party—support that soon helped bring both them and their new party out of the political wilderness and into statewide power. A tendency toward isolationism in foreign affairs was another enduring consequence.[66]

Passing Generations

"Thank God the war is over," wrote Anton Schmitt from Cold Spring to relatives in Germany as 1920 began. "But let's not talk anymore about war stories, it doesn't do any good."[67] That about summed up the attitude of most Minnesota Germans. German American associations may have changed their names and language usage during the war, but associational life itself determinedly continued. Thus in late 1917, St. Paul Germans formed a new *Spassvogel Verein* (jokers' club) that quickly became one of the city's largest and most active German clubs, performing German dramas to solidify group loyalties and raise money for postwar relief to Germany. The Old Heidelberg Club played a similar role in postwar Minneapolis. In November 1921 St. Paul's German community finally realized a 30-year-old dream with the opening of the Deutsches Haus (German House) on Rice Street, sponsored by some 51 of the city's 100–odd German lodges and associations as a central meeting place complete with bowling alleys, pool rooms, a

Minnesota Germans gathered for a Turnfest at Young America in 1914. Mass gymnastics exercises, along with individual and team competitions, were highpoints of periodic state and national Turner festivals that celebrated German ethnic culture.

Rathskeller, and a 1,000–seat theater. In Duluth groups like the Germania Singing Society, the Sons and Sisters of Hermann, the Turnverein, and the Eintracht working-men's society remained active in the interwar years. German old-time music expanded its audience when New Ulm's Whoopee John Wilfahrt began regular broadcasts on Twin Cities radio in 1924.[68] Catholic and Protestant churches throughout the state sent generous postwar relief to Germany, something they would also do after World War II.

Resistance to Prohibition represented another kind of ethnic assertion. Rural German areas, suffering agricultural hard times in the 1920s, often moved beyond basement home brew to moonshine "cooked" in barn or creekside stills. Legends gathered around premium products

Minnesota Moonshine

Nick Thelen was a farmer and sometime blacksmith near St. Stephens in Stearns County. As his son later recalled, "About 1922 financially times were getting harder and harder for father Nick. He was providing shelter, clothing and food for eleven people, plus all the feed for all the livestock. He decided he needed more income. He learned how to make moonshine from friends and neighbors and maybe over the fence at the back pasture. . . . We five boys rotated between distilling duties and the usual chores. Nick got into his Model T Ford and started scouting around the neighborhood saloons for prospective customers. . . . The moonshine was stored in charcoal barrels for a while for aging. Nick didn't like the color of the moonshine. It looked like water. So one day he heated a frying pan as hot as he could get it and dumped in some sugar and kept on stirring it until it formed into a brown liquid. This was add[ed] to the moonshine to give it the color of bourbon. This gave Nick a big sales advantage. One day while trying to sell to a saloon on St. Germain St. in St Cloud the feds caught up with him and put him in the county jail in St. Cloud. The penalty was 60 days in jail or a $200 fine. . . . We barely had enough money to get him out. He decided to continue in the business. It wasn't long and he got clobbered again. . . . Once the feds nailed someone they watched him like a peregrene (!) falcon. Nick tried his best to make a decent living for his large family, but it didn't work out and when he tried something else he got caught."

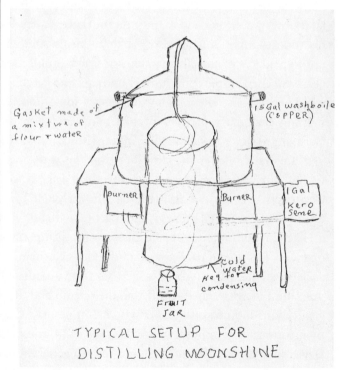

Robert Thielen illustrated his account of making moonshine with this drawing of a still.

like Stearns County's "Minnesota 13" (probably named for a corn hybrid) whose quality, it was said, came from the copper stills made by a sympathetic brother at St. John's Abbey. Local law enforcement frequently looked the other way, and if caught, "sitters" might return home from Leavenworth to a hero's welcome. By the late 1920s, as profits rose, volume increased, and outside money moved in, so did the 59 federal agents assigned to the Upper Midwest. They mounted a series of raids on Brown County and Winona area speakeasies and stills between 1928 and 1931, for example, boasting in June 1928 that "We did the same thing in St. Cloud and Stearns County. Now they are as tame as lambs there. They'll be the same in Winona before we're through." But they discounted the profit incentive; by October 1930, a new Stearns County crackdown on drugstores, speakeasies, soft drink parlors, beer farms, and homes netted 115 violators. As one Brown County resident later observed, he got a year and a day in Leavenworth for his moonshining, but he also got three farms south of Springfield.[69] But for all its folkloric legacy, Prohibition also weakened ethnic community bonds, pitting neighbor against neighbor, encouraging disrespect for authority, sapping customary patterns of sociability, and drawing Germans to share new national drinking habits.

Other factors led in the same direction. Postwar America had renewed appeal for immigrants from war-ravaged Germany like Duluth's Fritz Blaskoda, who arrived in 1923, found work at Fitger's Brewery, and together with his wife, a German domestic whom he met at citizenship class, opened a tavern and participated in the city's German associational life.[70] But restrictive laws after 1924 made immigration increasingly difficult, and the second and third generations loomed ever larger within Minnesota's German American community. In 1910, 28% of Minnesota's German-stock population (first and second generations) was foreign born; by 1930, that figure was only 18%, while

German Prisoner-of-War Camps

During World War II, more than 400,000 German prisoners of war were confined in more than 500 camps throughout the United States. About 1,275 of them were allocated from an Algona, Iowa, base camp to 20 camps in Minnesota at various times during 1944 and 1945 to help alleviate critical wartime labor shortages. They worked in lumber camps in the Chippewa National Forest, cutting pulpwood, clearing slash, and planting new trees. In southern Minnesota communities like Fairmont, Owatonna, New Ulm, and St. Charles, they picked peas and corn, worked in canneries, and did day-labor for farmers. In the Red River Valley, they worked on truck farms and helped with the beet and potato harvests. They lived in former CCC work camps, fairgrounds, and warehouses and factories converted to barracks. The Geneva Convention governed their treatment, and in the larger, more permanent camps they had baseball and volleyball fields, libraries and pianos, and even formed orchestras and classes. While fraternization between prisoners and locals was forbidden, it was difficult to enforce, particularly in German-speaking areas in the southern part of the state where local pastors provided German-language church services and farmers found themselves treating prisoners like hired hands. "We worked right along with them. We got along fine with them. They were fairly good workers considering the situation," remembered one Freeborn County farmer. An occasional prisoner went briefly AWOL, but the only serious escape attempt occurred in October 1944 when two prisoners from the Bena camp in the Chippewa National Forest tried to float down the Mississippi in a homemade boat. They traveled only 50 miles before they were caught five and a half days later. Most were content just to wait out the war. "It was a good school for me," one later recalled. "Not only were the Americans good workers, but good fellows." The last Minnesota camp, near Deer River, closed on December 26, 1945. Some spent as much as three more years in European labor camps before they made it back to Germany. A few would later return to settle permanently in Minnesota; more have come back to visit.

A group of prisoners-of war retuned from the day's work cutting logs and brush at the Deer River camp in March 1945.

the 17% decline of the state's German-stock population during those two decades, and the 6% decline of the second generation itself, points to the fading of family links with Germany.[71] Minnesota certainly welcomed some German Jewish refugees during the 1930s and a greater number of displaced persons from German-speaking areas of eastern Europe after World War II. By October 1951 more than 6,200 displaced persons, including many Germans, had been settled in Minnesota with the aid of religious and ethnic organizations and county agents who recruited them as farm labor. Ilsa Walz, for example, was expelled as a 15-year-old from the Sudetenland, escaped by night from an East German work camp into the West, and made her way to St. Joseph with the help of Catholic relief agencies. War brides like the 12 reported active in Duluth's International Institute in the late 1940s added another new element to Minnesota's post–World War II German population.[72] But for all practical purposes, German immigration had come to an end. The 2000 census found only 7,717 German born in Minnesota. Work, study, and family have continued to draw individual Germans to Minnesota, but changes in the state's German-ancestry population now largely reflect normal movements across state boundaries, ever-increasing intermarriage, and changing rates of ancestry identification.[73] Only the religious migration of Amish farmers after 1974 into Fillmore County, where they now support five church districts and seven one-room schools, and the seven Hutterite colonies (now numbering about 700 persons) established in western and southern Minnesota from South Dakota beginning in the late 1950s, have added new German communities to the state.[74]

Culture changed even more rapidly than the generations. By the 1920s the automobile, radio, telephone, and movies were already weakening rural isolation; Depression-era government programs and school consolidation helped speed the process. Agricultural modernization re-

The New Munich baseball team turned out fully equipped in 1931. By 1900 most Stearns County towns had baseball teams. The most enduring of the amateur leagues in the area was the Great Soo League, formed in 1926 by town teams along the Great Northern and Soo Line railroads, which lasted until 1965. Eugene McCarthy, who played for Watkins in the Great Soo League, remembered that in New Munich the cemetery was out in left field, so the trick was "to try to hit the ball among the headstones, figuring that the leftfielder wouldn't chance stepping on his grandfather's grave just to chase a ball. . . . In the Great Soo, that was considered place-hitting."

duced farm labor demand and slowly eroded the vitality of family farming, at the same time that military service, job opportunities, and the lure of city lights drew young people away. Post–World War II prosperity brought new consumption patterns and social norms into the countryside, while social mobility and suburbanization broke up old German neighborhoods in the cities. A 1935 survey found only 35 German societies remaining in St. Paul. By 1939 the Deutsches Haus was renting out its facilities and changed its name to the American House during the war (it was subsequently razed for the Capitol Approach). Most of the state's remaining German newspapers ceased publication by the early 1930s. St. Paul lost its German daily in 1941, the *Wanderer* changed to English at the end of 1944, and Minnesota's German press history finally ended in 1955 when Winona's Leicht publications moved to Omaha.[75] Familiar networks of family, friendship, religion, and community remained, but their German character seeped away. Just how far became evident during World War II: the FBI kept an eye on the state's remaining German societies, but only 27 of the nation's 6,362 wartime apprehensions of German Americans occurred in Minnesota.[76]

But even as the lived experience of ethnicity faded, new symbolic expressions of German heritage emerged, encouraged by renewed links to postwar Germany as a Cold War ally. Appropriately enough, given the role of public celebration in the initial emergence of German American ethnic identity, this took a festive form. Well before the national wave of interest in ethnic roots in the 1970s, Minnesota communities experimented with beery celebrations like New Ulm's Polka Day (1953–71) and Albany's G'Suffa Days (1960–68). St. Paul Germans founded their *Volksfest* Association (now the Germanic-American Institute) in 1956, acquiring a Summit Avenue headquarters a year later to house German language and culture classes, singing, dancing, and annual Oktoberfest and German Day celebrations. Both it and Richfield's German-American Fellowship Association of Minnesota, founded in 1961 as a chapter of D.A.N.K. (the German-American National Congress) and independent since 1972, maintain active cultural programs today; other groups cultivate German dancing, singing, and genealogy. New Ulm has refurbished its business street to reflect its German origins, and its

How to Make Sauerkraut

Many German children remember their mothers making sauerkraut—the labor, the smell, the look of the scum that rose to the top of the crock. In times before refrigeration, pickling, salting, smoking, drying, and canning kept food on the family table through the winter months. But even at the end of the 20th century, some women continued to make sauerkraut the old-fashioned way. Most followed a version of this basic recipe. Most followed a version of the basic recipe used by Rose Gohman of St. Joseph.

Take good sound heads of mature cabbage. Remove outside green and dirty leaves. Quarter the head and slice off the core. Shred the cabbage finely, sprinkle it with salt (about 5 pounds cabbage to 2 ounces salt). Pack gently into a crock with a potato masher. Repeat, layering cabbage sprinkled with salt until crock is full. Cover with a cloth, plate, and weight. Fermentation will be complete in 10 to 12 days. During the curing process, kraut requires daily attention. Remove the scum as it forms, and wash and scald the cloth often to keep it free from scum and mold. As soon as the kraut is thoroughly cured, pack into clean glass canning jars, adding enough of the kraut juice, or a weak brine made by dissolving 2 tablespoons salt to a quart of water, to fill jars within 1/2 inch of top. (One pound fits one pint glass jar.) Put on cap, screwing the band tight. Process in water bath for 15 minutes.

You don't need a German name to like sauerkraut! C. F. Whitford, winner of Henderson's 1936 sauerkraut-eating contest, is shown practicing for the 1948 Sauerkraut Days festival. Henderson's German-themed Sauerkraut Days goes back to the 1930s and continues today after an interruption in the 1970s.

From the 1930s onward, 75th anniversary and centennial celebrations encouraged Minnesota communities to remember their immigrant roots, and even as direct links with the homeland faded, summer festivals began to promote new forms of symbolic ethnicity. Here, New Ulm residents celebrate their 1954 centennial with a street dance to the music of one of the numerous German-style bands for which the city is noted.

Heritagefest, now in its 29th year, remains Minnesota's premier German celebration; newer festivals like St. Paul's Rheinfest (2001) and Emperor's Ball (2003) further underscore the renewed tug of German roots.[77] But the restoration of the distinctive German decorations and mottos in the State Capitol's rathskeller-style cafeteria (designed in 1905, painted over in 1917) in 1999, along with the renovation of New Ulm's Hermann, perhaps best embody the final public rehabilitation of Minnesota's once-discredited German heritage.

Nevertheless, for all the vows taken at its dedication, it is clear that the Hermann Monument today symbolizes ethnic memory and not enduring experience. A state is a porous net in which to capture memories. They weave back and forth across state boundaries like the immigrants themselves. Yet Minnesota shaped the experience of its German-origin population in distinctive ways, and Germans left enduring marks upon the state. The state's homestead lands gave its German population a larger church-oriented rural component, and a smaller proportion of urban workers and entrepreneurs, than in most other states. Disunity within the group combined with the Yankee-Scandinavian alliance within the dominant Republican Party to sideline Germans politically and culturally in

German culture has faded in Minnesota with the passing of generations, but its heritage remains in the memories and customs of Minnesota families and in the landscape itself. Among its most visible legacies are the church-centered villages like Pierz in Morrison County (shown here in 1970) that punctuate the Minnesota countryside and bear witness to the values and hopes that drew so many Germans to the state.

the 19th century and to keep them divided in the 20th. But their early arrival and numbers probably also ensured real economic opportunity and greater local control than in many other areas, helping to blunt the consequences of the First World War and to preserve ethnically derived family and community values even as awareness of their German origins faded. Traces of their legacy can be read in Minnesota's public culture today, in the prominent role of its faith-based communities, in the complex mix of conservative and liberal elements in its maverick politics, in its land ethic and careful business tradition. The traditional iron crosses in country graveyards may be crumbling, and old Germanic buildings may disappear in the name of progress. By one count, only 13 German restaurants are left in the state, and most of the old German crafts and customs have vanished. But families still preserve old photographs, cherished recipes, holiday rituals, ways of thinking and worshiping that are enduring links to the past. It is their stories, preserved in family memory and on ever-lengthening shelves of family histories in the libraries and historical societies of Minnesota, that are the best heritage and real history of German Minnesota.

Personal Account:
A Farmer in Stearns County

by George Kulzer

George Kulzer was born in 1831 near Moosbach in Bavaria's Oberpfalz. The unruly second son of poor farmers, he worked hard from childhood to help pay off family debts and at 18 fell in love with a pretty 16-year-old orphan, Margaritha Winter, whom he met in church. His parents disapproved; Margaritha earned her keep as a servant, and they wanted George to marry someone who would bring money to the farm. Indeed, a legal marriage was impossible without adequate funds. After four years his parents agreed to help them emigrate to America, but because he was liable for military service, he had to leave secretly. Sailing from Hamburg as brother and sister, they married in Pittsburgh in June 1854; their first child was born the following spring. Though George found work in an iron foundry, they wanted their own farm, and moved to Stearns County in June 1856. They were penniless when they staked out their claim and built their crude cabin in the "Indian forest" northwest of St. Joseph. Eventually their family included three girls and three boys. After several years of farming, George moved to Albany and opened a store and then a hotel. He also served on the local school board. He moved to Washington Territory with his second wife after Margaritha's 1885 death and later recalled those days in a memoir written shortly before his own death in 1912. We reproduce a selection from a literal translation by his daughter-in-law Mary Obermiller Kulzer that captures the spirit of the German original.

This was the turning point. I cant understand to this day how we lived through those times, but we did, and so it came that late in the fall a man by the name of Kochin started to build a flour mill near St. Joseph on Watab River. It was necessary to build a dam that took a lot of dirt digging and there I got work. I received 35¢ a day and had to board myself. It was small wages and a barrel of flour cost $16.00 and potatoes $2.50 a bushel, meat 25¢ a pound and lard 25¢ a pound, but tallow we could buy for 10¢ a pound. Cornmeal was not expensive so we bought cornmeal and tallow. We had to be contented with the cheaper articles. The cornmeal was then mixed with water. The pan was greased with tallow to keep the cornmeal from sticking to the pan. First one side was cooked and then the other and then eaten with a good apitite.

One incident that I must mention. That my wife could eat it better than I could, but hunger is the best cook and we had worked hard. We had to eat so we lived on that cornmeal, and had to like it. I worked about six weeks on that dam and then it was completed, but in the meantime my wife was not idle. She made use of the axe and grubhoe. She chopped small trees down, chopped down brush and piled it up and burned it. Then with the grubhoe she cultivated and hoed the ground so we could plant more vegetables the following spring. There was no prospect of work the rest of the year so we had to stretch what little we had from working on the dam to make it last during the winter and keep us from starving to death. My wife could cook much out of little and so we lived through the winter in hopes that the following year 1857, would be better, but in that we should be again sadly disappointed. Then the grasshoppers which had distroyed everything this year layed eggs in the ground so the next spring when the ground got warm the eggs hatched and so distroyed everything, even the leaves on the trees and the grass in the meadows. The ate everything. There was such a mass of them that they darkened the sun and when they were leaving they left as sudden as they came.

The first days in the year 1857 I learned to write again, so I rote a long letter to my parents and told them just exactly how everything was with us and what we were up against and asked them if at anytime there would be any money coming to me, that now was the time that we needed it. I must refer to the time when the winter was staring at us that fall. What will we do without a stove, but as usual my good wife always knew a way out and had a plan whereby we could get along without a stove. I was willing to do whatever she ordered me to do. She said "We will gather rocks and you build a large fireplace, we have plenty of wood and we can burn all we want. Then we wont freeze." We cooked over some rocks outside during the warm weather and baked bread in the oven I had built outside from loam, such as we used to build in the old country.

Well I did as I was told and we soon had enough rocks together so I started to build a big fireplace, bound the rocks together with loam, built a chiminy out of wood and loam. Now we had heat and light. We saved the dry wood for the evening so that would flare up and we had light in the house and we cooked in the fireplace. We had plenty of water as we dug a well in the fall 35 feet deep. I dug the dirt and my wife lifted the dirt in a pail. About half ways down I saw I was in great danger, I got in sand about 4 feet deep so I had to wall the hole with rails first before I could go any deeper.

Christmas day I went to church at St Joseph. We had errected a log building 20 x 24 and a missionery, Fr. Pierz was conducting a mission because the Benidictine priests who came the same time we did were still below St Cloud. . . .

In the spring a letter came from my parents and 300 Gulden or $120.00 in American money with that I went to Clearlake and bought a cow for $75.00 and I bought 2 for Zimmerman at the same time and one for $75.00 and one for $40.00, he had money. I also bought a stove for $32.00. So there was not much left of the $120.00, but now we had a cow and a stove to cook on. The cow soon b[r]ought us a calf, then we had milk and butter. We could now mix our cornmeal with milk, now and then, and grease the pan with butter. Then we had $13.00 left so I bought 100 pounds of flour and some more cornmeal. When the report reached the big cities that most of the emigrants were poor and the grasshoppers had eaten everything, they sent seed wheat as far as St Joseph. The poor people got 2 bushels, the others more. I took my 2 bushels on my shoulders and carried it home 3 miles[;] that's how I got everything else home, by carrying it on my back.

We planted the wheat on the ground we had cultivated the year before with a grub-hoe and grub[b]ed more land for corn, potatoes and cabbage. Everything came up and grew. It was a pleasure to see it, but it was not to last long, as again the grasshoppers ate everything when the warm weather set the eggs in the ground hatched and more numerous that the year before. Nothing was left. They destroyed everything.

So came the 14th of June and another daughter was born to us, we named her Barbara and as you can see the grasshoppers could not interfere with this crop. So now we had a little family, but it seemed after this as if God's blessing came with this crop. Work got more plentiful and I could get work off and on and so could buy the most necessary food. Even if the grasshoppers destroyed everything there was no danger of going hungry, but of course if mother, as I will call her from now on, had not been so saving or had not known how to manage it would still have been a scant living. I was lucky enough that fall to earn enough to buy a calf, a steer calf and we had one from our cow so there 2 steer calves should in the future be our span of oxen. Of course we had no plow or wagon in fact nothing but we lived in hopes and depended on God and trusted in him, but the time had not come when we could be too sure of our success.... By that time the year 1857 passed and we entered the year 1858. The spring of that year was nice and things began to look better. My oldest brother George Adam came from the old country and brought us $40.00 in money. Now we could buy ourselves some tools to work with, a grub-axe a shovel and a plow. We had no team yet but our future oxen were now a year old and 2 more years we could train them and hitch them to the plow and work them. My brother helped us with the work that spring and we build a better house. We split large oak logs and made a floor in the new house and a floor above, and then shingled the roof with shingles made out of oak logs, so now we had only a log house fit to live in. The crops were good that year but we had only a small patch of ground cleared so I went to work and during harvesting and my brother hired out to J. H. Linneman for a whole year so one can see that it went slowly forward. Now we felt safe from starvation. The danger was passed but many in our place would have said, "We have nothing yet," but we felt that we were farmers now.

From the George Kulzer Collection, Washington State University Libraries, Pullman, Wash.

For Further Reading

Conzen, Kathleen Neils. *Making Their Own America: Assimilation Theory and the German Peasant Pioneer.* New York: Berg, 1990.

Gjerde, Jon. *The Minds of the West: Ethnocultural Evolution in the Rural Middle West, 1830–1917.* Chapel Hill: University of North Carolina Press, 1997.

Glasrud, Clarence A., ed. *A Heritage Deferred: The German-Americans in Minnesota.* Moorhead, Minn.: Concordia College, 1981.

———. *A Heritage Fulfilled: German-Americans.* Moorhead, Minn.: Concordia College, 1984.

Holmquist, June D., ed. *They Chose Minnesota: A Survey of the State's Ethnic Groups.* St. Paul: Minnesota Historical Society Press, 1981.

Jaakkola, Terry, and Julia Lambert Frericks. *Shadows Illuminated: Women in a Rural Culture.* St. Cloud: Stearns County Historical Society, 1996.

Kamphoefner, Walter D., Wolfgang Helbich, and Ulrike Sommer. *News from the Land of Freedom: German Immigrants Write Home.* Ithaca: Cornell University Press, 1991.

Luebke, Frederick C. *Bonds of Loyalty: German-Americans and World War I.* DeKalb: Northern Illinois University Press, 1974.

Peterson, Fred W. *Building Community, Keeping the Faith: German Catholic Vernacular Architecture in a Rural Minnesota Parish.* St. Paul: Minnesota Historical Society Press, 1998.

Rippley, La Vern J., with Robert J. Paulson. *German-Bohemians: The Quiet Immigrants.* Northfield: St. Olaf College Press for the German-Bohemian Heritage Society, 1995.

Tolzmann, Don Heinrich. *The German-American Experience.* Amherst, N.Y.: Humanity Books, 2000.

Notes

1. Julius Schütze, "Fest-Rede gehalten zur Einweihung des Hermann's Denkmals, zu New Ulm, Minnesota, am 25. September, 1897," clipping in *Historische Ereignisse des Ordens der Hermanns-Söhne im State Minnesota,* scrapbook assembled by Adam Simmon, 1898, Minnesota Historical Society (hereafter MHS); on the statue and its dedication, see also Erich Sandow, "Das Hermannsdenkmal in New Ulm, Minnesota U.S.A.," *Mitteilungen aus der lippischen Geschichte und Landeskunde,* Sonderdruck, 25 (1956): 61–93. The monument was sponsored by the Sons of Hermann, a national fraternal order founded in 1840 and dedicated to the preservation of German culture in America.

2. For fuller tabulations of Germans in Minnesota censuses, see Hildegard Binder Johnson, "The Germans," in *They Chose Minnesota: A Survey of the State's Ethnic Groups,* ed. June Drenning Holmquist (St. Paul: Minnesota Historical Society Press, 1981), 158–59.

3. Friedrich Schmitz, Stillwater, Apr. 23, 1858, to his parents in Blankenheimerdorf, Rhine Province, typescript transcript, Germans in the United States Collection, box 1, State Historical Society of Wisconsin, Madison, Wisc. For summaries of recent scholarship on German emigration, see Dirk Hoerder, *Cultures in Contact: World Migrations in the Second Millennium* (Durham, N.C.: Duke University Press, 2002); Walter D. Kamphoefner, Wolfgang Helbich, and Ulrike Sommer, eds., *News from the Land of Freedom: German Immigrants Write Home* (Ithaca, N.Y.: Cornell University Press, 1991).

4. O. H. Rudnick, *Das Deutschtum St. Paul's in Wort und Bild* (St. Paul: Deutsche Theater, 1924), 7; Patricia C. Harpole and Mary D. Nagel, eds., *Minnesota Territorial Census, 1850* (St. Paul: Minnesota Historical Society, 1972); William P. Furlan, *In Charity Unfeigned: The Life of Father Francis Xavier Pierz* (St. Cloud: Diocese of St. Cloud, 1952); Leland R. Stevens, "Mission to the Chippewa," *Concordia Historical Institute Quarterly* 58 (1985): 117–35. Pierz was born in the Austrian province of Slovenia and came to the U.S. in 1835 at the age of 50 to work among the Indians of Michigan. See also John C. Massmann, "German Immigration to Minnesota, 1850–1890" (Ph.D. diss., University of Minnesota, 1966), for a basic account of Minnesota's German peopling.

5. Harpole and Nagel, eds., *Minnesota Territorial Census, 1850.*

6. Rudnick, *Das Deutschtum St. Paul's in Wort und Bild, 7;* Francois Martin, "Aus dem Nordwesten: Lose Blätter aus Minnesota's Geschichte," Scrapbook of Newspaper Clippings, MHS; T. M. Newson, *Pen Pictures of St. Paul, Minnesota, and Biographical Sketches of Old Settlers* (St. Paul, 1886), 103–4 (quote 103).

7. Harpole and Nagel, eds., *Minnesota Territorial Census, 1850;* http://www.historyontheweb.org/minnbrew/mnbrew.html

8. John A. Diethelm, *The History of St. Victoria Parish, 1857–1957* (St. Cloud: Sentinel Publishing Co., 1957).

9. Jessie C. Davis, *Beaver Bay: Original North Shore Village* (Duluth: St. Louis County Historical Society, 1968); Esther

Abbetmeyer Selke, "Two Interesting Visitors in St. Paul During August, 1856," 4 (1931): 37–43, "The Beginnings of the German Lutheran Churches in Minnesota," 2 (1930), 108–15, "Herculean Laborers for the Extension of Lutheranism in Minnesota," 4 (1931), 79–87—all *Concordia Historical Institute Quarterly; Centennial 1857–1957, Zion Lutheran Church* (Cologne, Minn.,1957); *Fuenfzig-Jaehriges Jubilaeum 1871–1921, Luth. St. Johannis-Gemeinde* (Helen Township, McLeod County) (Glencoe, Minn.: Republic Print, 1921), 2, 5.

10. J. B. Tennelly, trans., "Father Pierz, Missionary and Colonizer," in *Acta et Dicta*, 7:129 (October 1935); Kathleen Neils Conzen, *Making Their Own America: Assimilation Theory and the German Peasant Pioneer* (New York: Berg, 1990); Ireland's assessment appears in *Acta et Dicta*, 2:278 (July 1910).

11. Hildegard B. Johnson, "The Founding of New Ulm, Minnesota," *American-German Review* (June 1946), 8–12; Noel Iverson, *Germania, U.S.A.: Social Change in New Ulm, Minnesota* (Minneapolis: University of Minnesota Press, 1966). See Johnson, "The Germans," for a fuller account.

12. See Johnson, "The Germans."

13. Carlton C. Qualey, "Russian Germans," typescript, box 10, Minnesota Ethnic History Project Records, 1969–1982 (hereafter MEHP), MHS. Seeger was impeached and removed from office shortly thereafter.

14. Hubert Neumann, Bird Island, Renville Co., to "Lieber Vater und Geschwister," Feb. 4, 1885, box 1, Germans in the United States Collection.

15. Table 8.3, Johnson, "The Germans," 164.

16. United States, *Census, 1880, Population*, 714, 730, 752.

17. Hildegard Binder Johnson, "Germans," typescript, box 9, MEHP.

18. Conzen, *Making Their Own America*, 11–12.

19. La Vern J. Rippley with Robert J. Paulson, *German-Bohemians: The Quiet Immigrants* (Northfield, Minn.: St. Olaf College Press for the German-Bohemian Heritage Society, 1995). Berghold's German-language guidebook to Minnesota was published in 1876.

20. http://www.unke-genealogy.de; "Biography of Herman F. Kuschel," recorded for the Morrison County Historical Society, June 1937, in WPA Papers—Stearns County, box 3, MHS.

21. Johnson, "The Germans," 163–64.

22. C[arl] M[athias] Klein, *The History of Millerville, Douglas County, Minnesota, 1866 to 1930* (Millerville: Klein Co. Store, 1930), 81.

23. Kamphoefner, Helbich, and Sommer, eds., *News from the Land of Freedom*, 226.

24. Conzen, *Making Their Own America*.

25. Franklyn Curtiss-Wedge, ed., *History of Dakota and Goodhue Counties, Minnesota* (Chicago: H. C. Cooper, Jr., 1910), 2:379–80.

26. Charles Edwin Dick, "A Geographical Analysis of the Development of the Brewing Industry of Minnesota" (Ph.D. diss., University of Minnesota, 1981).

27. John T. Flanagan, *Theodore Hamm in Minnesota: His Family and Brewery* (Minneapolis: Pogo Press, 1989); Dick, "Geographical Analysis," 160.

28. William B. Mitchell, *History of Stearns County, Minnesota* (Chicago: H. C. Cooper, Jr., 1915), 76.

29. "Large Midwestern Woolen Mill Founded by German Cabinetmaker," *America's Textile Reporter*, June 8, 1961, copy in MEHP, box 10; http://www.northernhardwoodinc.com/staff.htm.

30. Julie Hiller Schrader, *The Heritage of Blue Earth County, Minnesota* (Dallas: Curtis Media Corp., 1990), 301.

31. For more on the Weyerhaeuser family, see Charles E. Twining, *F. K. Weyerhaeuser: A Biography* (St. Paul: Minnesota Historical Society Press, 1997).

32. LaVern J. Rippley, "German-American Banking in Minnesota," 94–115, and Clarence A. Glasrud, "Introduction," 12–15, in *A Heritage Fulfilled: German-Americans*, ed. Clarence A. Glasrud (Moorhead: Concordia College, 1984); Gretchen Leisen, *The John Zapp and Margaretha Hoffmann Legacy: A Family History and Genealogy of the Zapp, Hoffmann and Theisen Families of Stearns County* (St. Cloud: Continental Press, 1989); *St. Paul Pioneer Press*, Sept. 16, 1997.

33. John C. Massmann, "Mathilda Tolksdorf and Daniel Shillock: A German-American Frontier Family Experience," in *Heritage Fulfilled*, 196–210.

34. Mary Lethert Wingerd, *Claiming the City: Politics, Faith, and the Power of Place in St. Paul* (Ithaca, N.Y.: Cornell University Press, 2001); Johnson, "The Germans," 168–70; Newson, *Pen Pictures*, 637.

35. Wingerd, *Claiming the City*; George W. Lawson, *History of Labor in Minnesota* (St. Paul: Minnesota State Federation of Labor, 1955); Steve Leikin, "The Cooperative Coopers of Minneapolis," *Minnesota History* 57 (Winter 2001–02), 386–405; Union Advocate Labor History Series, http://www.workdayminnesota.org.

36. Colman J. Barry, *Worship and Work* (Collegeville: Liturgical Press, 1980).

37. Statistics calculated from the listings in Johannes Nep. Enzlberger, ed., *Schematismus der katholischen Geistlichkeit deutscher Zunge in den Vereinigten Staaten Amerikas* (Milwaukee: Hoffmann Brothers Co., 1892).

38. Vincent A. Yzermans, *Frontier Bishop of St. Cloud* (Waite Park, Minn.: Park Press, 1988); Daniel P. O'Neill, "The Development of a German-American Priesthood: The Benedictines and St. Paul Diocesan Clergy, 1851–1930," in *Heritage Fulfilled*, 145–55.

39. Sister M. Grace McDonald, *With Lamps Burning* (St. Joseph, Minn.: St. Benedict's Priory Press, 1957).

40. Calculated from Enzlberger, ed., *Schematismus*.

41. Conzen, *Making Their Own America*; Sister Nora Luetmer, *The History of Catholic Education in the Present Diocese of St. Cloud, Minnesota, 1855–1965* (Ph.D. diss., University of Minnesota, 1966); Vincent A. Yzermans, *The Spirit in Central Minnesota* (St. Cloud: Diocese of St. Cloud, 1989), 2:553.

42. Conzen, *Making Their Own America*; John S. Kulas, *Der Wanderer of St. Paul: The First Decade, 1867–1877* (New York: Peter Lang, 1996); Vincent A. Yzermans, *With Courage and Hope: The Catholic Aid Association, 1878–1978* (St. Paul: Catholic Aid Assn., 1978); Enzlberger, *Schematismus*.

43. Karl J. Fink, "German Lutherans in Minnesota," in *Heritage Fulfilled*, 156–67; Susan Diebold, "Germans-Protestants," typescript in MEHP, box 10; Esther Abbetmeyer-Selke, "The Beginnings of the German Lutheran Churches in Minnesota," *Concordia Historical Institute Quarterly* 2 (1929): 75–81, 108–15 (1924 statistics, 115).

44. In addition to the references above, see *Centennial, 1857–1957* (Cologne, Minn.: Zion Lutheran Church, 1957); *Fuenfzig-Jaehriges Jubilaeum, 1871–1921* (Helen Township, McLeod County: Luth. St. Johannis-Gemeinde, 1921); Brent T. Peterson and Dean R. Thilgen, *Cornerstones: 125 Years at St. Paul Lutheran Church, Stillwater, Minnesota* (Stillwater: Valley History Press, 1996); *History of Immanuel Lutheran Congregation* (Cass Lake, Minn.: The Congregation, 1932); Paul Marschke, "German Lutherans in Minnesota: Glimpses into the Americanization of a City Parish, 1890–1940," *Lutheran Historical Conference: Essays and Reports,* 11:14–38.

45. Diebold, "Germans-Protestants," MEHP, box 10; see Johnson, "The Germans," 170–72, for more detail.

46. Quoted from the *New Ulm Pionier,* 1858, in Iverson, *Germania, U.S.A.,* 67.

47. Johnson, "The Germans," 172; Margaret Mussgang, "The Germans in St. Paul" (master's thesis, University of Minnesota, 1932), 73–85.

48. Martin, "Aus dem Nordwesten"; Johnson, "The Germans," 172; Mussgang, "Germans in St. Paul," 65; tabulation of German organizations listed in R. L. Polk & Co., *St. Paul City Directory, 1890–91.*

49. Thomas James Wenberg, *Violin and Bow Makers of Minnesota* (St. Paul: Schubert Club Museum, 1988); quotation cited in Kathleen Neils Conzen, "Ethnicity and Musical Culture among the German Catholics of the Sauk, 1854–1920," in Philip Bohlman and Otto Holzapfel, *Land without Nightingales: Music in the Making of German-America* (Madison: University of Wisconsin Press, 2002).

50. Conzen, "Ethnicity and Musical Culture"; LaVern J. Rippley, *The Whoopee John Wilfahrt Dance Band: His Bohemian-*

German Roots (Northfield: St. Olaf College German Dept., 1992), 31–71.

51. Annemarie Springer, *Nineteenth Century German-American Church Artists* (Bloomington, Ind.: The author, 2001), at http://www.ulib.iupui.edu/kade/springer/index.html, Ch. 6, p. 3; *Stones and Hills, Steine und Huegel* (Collegeville: St. John the Baptist Parish, 1975), 34–35; Peter Eich obituary, *Nordstern* (St. Cloud), Dec. 16, 1920; Rena Neumann Coen, *Painting and Sculpture in Minnesota, 1820–1914* (Minneapolis: University of Minnesota Press, 1976). More central were later German American arrivals on the Minnesota art scene, such as Munich-trained Robert Koehler, who became director of the Minneapolis School of Art in 1894, and second- and third-generation artists like Wanda Gág and Adolf Dehn.

52. David Gebhard and Tom Martinson, *A Guide to the Architecture of Minnesota* (Minneapolis: University of Minnesota Press, 1977); Mary E. Nilles, *Rollingstone;* Steven Cleo Martens, "Ethnic Tradition and Innovation as Influences on a Rural, Midwestern Building Vernacular: Findings from Investigation of Brick Houses in Carver County, Minnesota" (master's thesis, University of Minnesota, 1988); Fred W. Peterson, *Building Community, Keeping the Faith: German Catholic Vernacular Architecture in a Rural Minnesota Parish* (St. Paul: Minnesota Historical Society Press, 1998); Schrader, *Heritage of Blue Earth County,* 101–2, 512.

53. Johnson, "The Germans," 173–74; Gerhard H. Weiss, "The German Language Press in Minnesota," in *Heritage Fulfilled,* 47–63.

54. Carl H. Chrislock, "The German-American Role in Minnesota Politics,

1850–1950," in *A Heritage Deferred: The German-Americans in Minnesota,* Clarence A. Glasrud, ed. (Moorhead: Concordia College, 1981), 104–16; http://www.minnesotapolitics.net.

55. Hildegard Binder Johnson, "The Election of 1860 and the Germans in Minnesota," *Minnesota History* 28 (March 1947): 20–36.

56. Calculated from regiment rosters and biographies compiled at http//www.firstminnesota.com.

57. Kevin J. Weddle, "Ethnic Discrimination in Minnesota Volunteer Regiments during the Civil War," *Civil War History* 35 (1989): 239–59.

58. Civil War Military and Pension Records, U.S. National Archives, Washington, D.C.

59. Kathleen Neils Conzen, "German Catholic Communalism and the American Civil War: Exploring the Dilemmas of Transatlantic Political Integration," in *Bridging the Atlantic: The Question of American Exceptionalism in Perspective,* Elisabeth Glaser and Hermann Wellenreuther, eds. (Cambridge: Cambridge University Press, 2002), 119–44.

60. Kathleen Neils Conzen, "German-Americans and Ethnic Political Culture: Stearns County, Minnesota, 1855–1915," Working Paper Series No. 16, John F. Kennedy Institute for North American Studies, Free University of Berlin, 1989; Conzen, "German Catholic Communalism"; *Nordstern,* Oct. 12, 1876 (quote). For local politics in action, see Stephen J. Gross, "The Battle Over the Cold Spring Dam: Farm-Village Conflict and Contested Identity among Rural German Americans," *Journal of American Ethnic History* 21 (2001): 83–117.

61. Joseph Matt, "The Catholic City Federation of St. Paul," in *Acta et Dicta* 7: 95–103 (1935).

62. Nov. 1, 1916, quoted in Carl H. Chrislock, *The Progressive Era in Minnesota, 1899–1918* (St. Paul: Minnesota Historical Society, 1971), 98; see also Johnson's discussion of this era in "The Germans," 175–77.

63. Quoted in Chrislock, *Progressive Era,* 143.

64. Johnson, "The Germans," 175–77 and the references cited there; Carl H. Chrislock, *Watchdog of Loyalty: The Minnesota Commission of Public Safety During World War I* (St. Paul: Minnesota Historical Society Press, 1991); Frederick L. Johnson, *Goodhue County, Minnesota: A Narrative History* (Red Wing: Goodhue County Historical Society, 2000), 203–12; Corrine McCarthy, "The Treatment of German-Americans in Montgomery, Minnesota, during World War I" (master's proseminar essay, Hamline University, 1998).

65. Chrislock, *Watchdog of Loyalty,* and "German-American Role"; Donald Tolzmann, "The German Language Press in Minnesota, 1855 to 1955," *German-American Studies* 5 (1972): 176; Johnson, "Germans in Minnesota"; Yzermans, *Spirit in Central Minnesota,* 244–47; Diebold, "German Lutherans"; William L. Cofell, "A Report of a Research Project in a Benedictine Rural Parish," 1955, copy in author's possession; Lowry Nelson, *The Minnesota Community: Country and Town in Transition* (Minneapolis: University of Minnesota Press, 1960), 44–45; Heinz Kloss, "Die Stellung des Deutschen Elements in den Abstammungs- und Spracherzählungen der Jahre 1969–80," in *Deutsche als Muttersprache in den Vereinigten Staaten,* vol. 2 (Wiesbaden: Franz Steiner Verlag, 1985).

66. Stephen John Gross, "German-Americans and the Populist Appeal: The 1918 Elections in Stearns County," undergraduate paper, Department of History, University of Minnesota, 1984; Mary Lethert Wingerd, "The Americanization of Cold Spring: Cultural Change in an Ethnic Community," honors thesis, Macalester College, 1990. Prohibition complicated the politics of revenge in the 1920s and early 1930s, with Germans often voting for "wet" candidates regardless of party; the prominence of "dry" Scandinavians in Farmer-Laborism was a perennial source of suspicion among Germans.

67. Anton Schmitt, Cold Spring, Minn., Jan. 2, 1920, to Matthias Schmitt, Engeln, Germany, box 2, Germans in the United States Collection.

68. Rudnick, *Das Deutschtum St. Paul's in Wort und Bild;* Hildegard Binder Johnson, "Germans" typescript, and interview summary, Mr. and Mrs. Fritz Blaskoda, Duluth, MEHP; Rippley, *German-Bohemians,* 234. See William L. Cofell's comments on the persisting "halt's maul" (hold your tongue) attitude of German Americans in "The Motives of German Immigration," *Heritage Deferred,* 120.

69. William G. Shepherd, "Under Mr. Volstead's Nose," *Collier's,* Mar. 16, 1929, p. 8–9, 75–76; *Stones and Hills,* 117, quoting Fr. Godfrey Diekmann, OSB; Vincent A. Yzermans, *The Mel and the Rose* (Melrose: Melrose Historical Society, 1972), 239–43, 263–65; Lois Thelen, *Freeport: 100 Years of Family, Faith, and Fortune* (Freeport, 1992), 11–15; John Keane, "Prohibition Enforcement in Winona," term paper, St. Mary's College, Dec. 14, 1977, copy in MHS (quote); Steven Maras, "Prohibition in Brown County," typescript, June 7, 1976, copy in MHS (interview); John J. Do-minik, Jr., *Three Towns into One City: St. Cloud, Minnesota* (St. Cloud: Stearns County Historical Society, 1988), 57–60.

70. Blaskoda interview.

71. U.S., *Census,* 1910, *Population,* 1:837, 894; U.S., *Census,* 1939, *Population,* vol. 3, pt. 1, 1194.

72. Press release, Oct. 31, 1951, Displaced Persons Commission, Washington, D.C., in "Germans-Displaced Persons" file, box 9, MEHP; Idelia Loso, *St. Joseph: Preserving a Heritage* (St. Cloud: Sentinel Printing Co., 1989), 173–74; "Germans—Duluth & North Shore" file, box 9, MEHP.

73. http://factfinder.census.gov/servlet/BasicFactsServlet; one measure of cumulative intermarriage: 59% of the Minnesotans who specified German ancestry on the 1990 census listed another ancestry as well.

74. http://www.bluffcountry.com/villagegreen.htm/; "Minnesota Hutterites Continue to Thrive," *The Forum* (Fargo), Aug. 19, 2001, p. A10; John Movius, "Hutterite Place Names in North America—1997 Schmiedeleut Colonies List," http://feefhs.org/hut/1997/h-s1997.html; William Schroeder and Helmut T. Huebert, *Mennonite Historical Atlas,* 2 ed. (Winnipeg, Man.: Springfield Publishers, 1996), 153.

75. "Recreation Survey of St. Paul, Minn., 1934," typescript, box 10, MEHP; Tolzmann, "German Language Press"; J. R. Arndt and May E. Olson, eds., *German-American Newspapers and Periodicals, 1732–1955: History and Bibliography* (New York: Johnson Reprint Corp., 1965), 1:220.

76. Jewish Community Relations Council Papers, MHS; Don Heinrich Tolzmann, ed., *German Americans in the World Wars* (Munich: K. G. Saur, 1995), 4:1514–15.

77. Rippley, *German-Bohemians*, 243; Albany Heritage Society, *Albany: The Heart of Minnesota* (Albany, 1991), 167–68; Paul A. Schons, "German Clubs and Social Organizations," *Heritage Fulfilled*, 133–41; http://www.gai-mn.org and links; *Star Tribune* (Minneapolis), Jan. 3, 2000. The origins of Young America's three-day Stiftungsfest go back to the annual picnic of its Pioneer Maennerchor, founded in 1861; http://www.stiftungsfest.org.

Notes to Sidebars

A Frontier Company Town, p. 14: Donald Empson, *A History of the Dutchtown Residential Area, Stillwater, Minnesota* (Stillwater: Heritage Preservation Commission, 1998); Donald Empson, *A History of the South Half of the Carli & Schulenburg Addition Residential Area, Stillwater, Minnesota* (Stillwater: Heritage Preservation Commission, 2001).

Courtship, p. 30: Nordstern, Dec. 18, 1876.

Two Generations of Businesswomen, p. 39: Virginia L. Martin, "Giesen's, Costumers to St. Paul's Families and Fests, 1872–1970: A Ninety-year Run," *Ramsey County History* 28 (Winter 1994): 4–15.

"Carneval," p. 53: St. Paul Daily Pioneer Press, Feb. 27, Mar. 1, 1870 (quotations); *Minnesota Staats-Zeitung* (St. Paul), thrice weekly edition, Jan. 27–Mar. 1, 1870; Martin, "Aus dem Nordwesten"; *St. Cloud Times,* Feb. 4, 1871, Feb. 17, 1872, Feb. 26, 1873, Feb. 11, 1874.

Cultivating Minnesota's Garden, p. 58: Michael Heinz, "Botanical Exploration of Minnesota's Prairies: 1838–39, Carl Andreas Geyer," *Minnesota Plant Press* 8 (3),

Spring 1989; Dennis A. Gimmestad, "Territorial Space: Platting New Ulm," *Minnesota History* 56 (Summer 1999): 345–50; University of Minnesota Extension Service, "A History of Minnesota Floriculture," http://www.extension.umn.edu/distribution/horticulture/; http://www.angelfire.com/mn/thursdaynighthikes/irvine_arch2.html; Hennepin Parks, "Noerenberg Gardens on Lake Minnetonka," brochure; Ann Marie Johnson, "Munsinger and Clemens Gardens," *Crossings* (Stearns County Historical Society), 24 (Sept. 1998), 3–6.

"Fackel-Ludvigh," p. 60: Robert E. Cazden, *A Social History of the German Book Trade in America to the Civil War* (Columbia, S.C.: Camden House, 1984), 547–80.

A Civil War Soldier's Wife, p. 65: Adjutant General, Civil War Records, Box 4, General Correspondence, 1861–65, Minnesota State Archives, MHS (translation by author).

Looking for Disloyalty, p. 67: Photocopy of typescript from Minnesota Commission of Public Safety files, in "Germans," MEHP.

Minnesota Moonshine, p. 73: Robert D. Thielen, "Addendum, August 18, 1993," to "Memories of Robert D. Thielen, Country Doctor," 1988, copy in MHS.

German Prisoner-of-War Camps, p. 75: Anita Albrecht Buck, *Behind Barbed Wire: German Prisoners of War in Minnesota during World War II* (St. Cloud: North Star Press, 1998); George H. Lobdell, "Minnesota's 1944 PW Escape: Down the Mississippi in the *Lili Marlene #10*," *Minnesota History* 54 (Fall 1994): 112–23.

How to Make Sauerkraut, p. 79: Rose Gohman, quoted in Loso, *St. Joseph,* 230–31.

Index

Page numbers in italic refer to pictures and captions.

Schubert Club, 52, 54

Schulenburg, Frederick, 14

Schulenburg-Boeckeler sawmills, 14, *14*

Schwarzhoff brewery, *33*

Seebach, John C., 68

Seppman, Louis, 57

Settlement patterns, 5, 6; Amish farmers,
76; Catholics, 41–46; census, 4–5, 7,
13, 25; chain migration, 10, 18–19;
Hutterite colonies, 76; Lutherans, 20,
47–48; Protestants, 50; westward migration, 11–12

Shillock, Daniel, 37

Siebert, George, *54*

Sievers, Ferdinand, 13, 19–20

Spassvogel Verein (jokers' club), 71

Stahlmann, Christopher, *40*

Stearns County: baseball teams, *77*;
Catholic parishes and schools, 42–44;
Kulzer account, 83–86; local government officials, 65–66; Prohibition era,
74; settlement patterns, 20–21, 26–27

Stein, Peter, 13

Strauss, John, Sr. and Jr., *37*

Strauss Skate Shop, *37*

Tauer, Celia, *32*

Tivoli Concert Hall, *62*

Trinity Lutheran congregation, St. Paul,
47

Trott, Hermann, 23

Turnverein (Turner movement), *x*, 51,
72, *72*

Urban life, *see* individual cities

Volksfest Association, 78

Walz, Ilsa, 76

Weyerhaeuser, Frederick, 36

Whitford, C. F., *79*

Wieland brothers, 19

Wieland Lumber Company, *19*

Wilfahrt, Whoopee John, 72

Willius, Ferdinand and Gustav, *11*, 36

Wingerd, Mary Lethert, 39

Winona County, 26

Wirth, Theodore, 58

Wolff, Albert, 23, 59

Women: occupations and employment,
31–32, *32*, *38*; Turnverein, *x*; war
brides, 76

World War I: actions against German
community, 67–71; patriotic rally, *70*

World War II, 78; prisoner-of-war camps,
75

Yoerg, Anthony, 16, 32

Young America, *49*, 95n77; Turnfest, *72*

Zapp, John, 37

Picture Credits

Names of the photographers, when known, and source information are in parentheses.

Front cover: courtesy Sally Thomte, Roseville, Minn.

Page x (Charles P. Gibson), 2, 8, 11 (John Runk; Rippley, "German-American Banking"), 15 (Newson, *Pen Pictures*, 37–38), 18 (Henry A. Briol; *Albany: The Heart of Minnesota*, 52), 19 (Charles Alfred Zimmerman; Hugh E. Bishop, *By Water and Rail: A History of Lake County, Minnesota* [Duluth: Lake Superior Port Cities, 2000], 11–15), 21, 24 (Paul's Studio, Jackson, Minn.), 27 (*Stones and Hills*, 71; *Nordstern*, Dec. 11, 1919), 28, 31, 32, 33 (Charles S. Bryant, *History of Houston County* [Minneapolis: Minnesota Historical Co., 1882], 333–41), 34 (Alfred Palmquist; Flanagan, *Theodore Hamm in Minnesota*), 36 (James E. Carroll "Oscar Claussen, M. Am. Soc. C.E.: died October 26, 1932" [N.p.: American Society of Civil Engineers, 1932]), 37 (*St. Paul Pioneer Press*, Oct. 18, 1946, p. 13), 38, 40 (Newson, *Pen Pictures*, 331; Dick, "Geographical Analysis"), 41, 43, 44 (Runk; Enzlberger, ed., *Schematismus*, 285; Donald J. Layden, *100 Years, St. Mary's Parish, Stillwater, Minnesota* [Stillwater, 1965]), 46, 48 (Edward C. Fredrich, *The Wisconsin Synod Lutherans* [Milwaukee: Northwestern Pub. House, 1992]), 49, 52, 53 (top, Charles Alfred Zimmerman), 54 (Thomas J. Wenberg, *Violin and Bow Makers of Minnesota* [St. Paul: Schubert Club Museum, 1988]), 55 (Gebhard and Martinson, *A Guide to the Architecture of Minnesota*), 56 (http://www.spengler.li/otto/emigration_eng/.htm; Martens, "Ethnic Tradition"), 57 (Jacoby; Kenneth Carley, *The Dakota War of 1862* [St. Paul: Minnesota Historical Society Press, 1976], 37), 59 (*St. Paul Pioneer Press*, June 30, 1968), 60 (*Der Deutsche Pionier* [Cincinnati, Ohio], February 1870, frontispiece), 61, 62 (*Northwest Magazine*, February 1889, p. 9), 64 (Joel Whitney; http://www.firstminnesota.com), 69 (Anita Rapone, *The Guardian Life Insurance Company, 1860–1920: A History of a German-American Enterprise* [New York: New York University Press, 1987]), 70 (Henry Briol; "Loyalty in Stearns County during the Great War," *Crossings* 24 [1998]), 72, 75 (*Minneapolis Tribune*, March 4, 1945), 77 (Briol Studio; "Take Me Out to the Ball Game," *Stearns County Historical Society Newsletter* 6 [1980]; Eugene J. McCarthy, "My Life in the Great Soo League," in *Gene McCarthy's Minnesota: Memories of a Native Son* [Minneapolis: Winston Press, 1982], 69), 79 (*Mankato Free Press*, Dec. 30, 1999), 80 (*Minneapolis Star*, August 17, 1954), 81 (Vincent H. Mart)—all Minnesota Historical Society.

Acknowledgments

This essay builds on, revises, and expands the late Hildegard Binder Johnson's chapter, "The Germans," in *They Chose Minnesota;* her path-breaking research remains an invaluable resource for anyone interested in Minnesota's German past. The author would also like to thank Elaine Collins, Michael Conzen, Loretta Neils, Debbie Miller, Rebecca Rubinstein, Sally Rubinstein, and Christopher Winter for their assistance.

Minnesotans can trace their families and their state's heritage to a multitude of ethnic groups. *The People of Minnesota* series tells each group's story in a compact, handsomely illustrated, and accessible paperback. Readers will learn about the group's accomplishments, ethnic organizations, settlement patterns, and occupations. Each book includes a personal story of one person or family, told through a diary, a letter, or an oral history.

In his introduction to the series, Bill Holm reminds us why these stories are as important as ever: "To be ethnic, somehow, is to be human. Neither can we escape it, nor should we want to. You cannot interest yourself in the lives of your neighbors if you don't take sufficient interest in your own."

This series is based on the critically acclaimed book *They Chose Minnesota: A Survey of the State's Ethnic Groups* (Minnesota Historical Society Press). The volumes in *The People of Minnesota* bring each group's story up to date and add dozens of photographs to inform and enhance the telling.

Books in the series include *Irish in Minnesota*, *Jews in Minnesota*, *Norwegians in Minnesota*, *African Americans in Minnesota* and *Germans in Minnesota*.

Bill Holm is the grandson of four Icelandic immigrants to Minneota, Minnesota, where he still lives. He is the author of eight books including *Eccentric Island: Travels Real and Imaginary* and *Coming Home Crazy*. When he is not practicing the piano or on the road circuit-riding for literature, he teaches at Southwest State University in Marshall, Minnesota.

About the Author

Kathleen Neils Conzen is a professor of American history at the University of Chicago. She is the author of *Immigrant Milwaukee, 1836–1860: Accommodation and Community in a Frontier City* and *Making Their Own America: Assimilation Theory and the German Peasant Pioneer.*